Institutions Are People

Institutions Are People

JOHN DAY BOOKS IN

S E

SPECIAL EDUCATION

E. CHARLES BAUER

A DOCUMENTARY OF LIFE IN A STATE SCHOOL FOR THE MENTALLY RETARDED

The John Day Company
New York

Library of Congress Catalogue

Card Number: 66-25074

PRINTED IN THE UNITED STATES OF AMERICA

Dedicated

to

All Those People

AND WITH DEEP GRATITUDE TO OTHER PEOPLE
LIKE
THERESA MUSSO, K. THOMAS FINLEY, AND GAIL MURRAY

By the same author

A Graphichism of Christian Doctrine
Retarded Children Are People
Instant Theology

AUTHOR'S NOTE: *While the facts in this story are from the actual experiences of the writer, the identities of all patients have been concealed by the use of fictitious names, and any resemblance to persons living or dead is purely coincidental.*

Any financial return to the author from his books is to be used for the sole purpose of the construction of a chapel for the Catholic patients at the Newark State School in the State of New York.

PREFACE

STATE institutions for the retarded have shifted their program emphasis in recent years toward more training and treatment programming and less custodial care. A greater proportion of those admitted have been people with other serious problems, medical and emotional, in addition to retardation. Institution personnel have thought more in terms of helping the family and community with major problems where retardation is involved, with planning for return of the individual to his home and family when the major problems have been dealt with. As a result, there is greater concern with a closer working relationship of the institution with the families and communities it is serving. A better understanding of the institution, its personnel, and its policies is vital. This documentary can do much to help those on the outside see those on the inside with their concerns and objectives.

At about the same time as this program shift there has come a larger role for the Chaplain and his religious programs. Once seen as an outsider, meeting only certain religious needs, the Chaplain has become a member of the training and treatment team. His programs have become a more vital part of the total institutional program as it has been recognized that a good religious program has many practical, immediate values in addition to its primary spiritual goal. A good religious program helps give the retarded a more constructive self-concept, gives them hope, helps them experience the love of God and of His concerned fellowman, gives them moral guidance and a stable standard of values, helps relieve anxiety and guilt, has socialization values, and helps them build more constructive attitudes toward authority figures, toward the world in which they live, and toward one another. Some of these added benefits may be seen in Father Bauer's accounts.

Mental retardation is no respecter of race, religion, or social class. What is written in this book may be multiplied many times in institutions in different states and by Chaplains of different faiths. This is a typical delineation of the nature and problems of the retarded, the concerns of those who work with them, the significance of their faith to them, and their responsiveness to their religion. This book is significant because it is typical. May God use it to deepen the understanding, concern, and cooperation of all who have to do with the problems of mental retardation.

V. G. MOSTROM

Protestant Chaplain
Woodward State Hospital and School
Woodward, Iowa

Chairman, Chaplains' Sub-section
American Association on Mental Deficiency

CONTENTS

CONTENTS

Institutions Are People

I

A WARM RECEPTION

I LIVE in an institution. Not by choice. I was not put away by my family. I have not been committed by the court. I did not sign myself in. I am not here to be trained, rehabilitated, cured, punished, or kept out of circulation.

I am here to work. I was sent here by my superior. I am paid by the people of the state. I was assigned and am being paid to minister to souls. That is what my superior and the people of this state expect me to do. So does God, whom they represent.

But that is not what this institution is for. There is an institution designed to minister to souls—the Church. I belong to that institution, too. The one I *live* in is different—different from the Church, but *not* different from any other institution (used in the distasteful sense of that word, in which we speak of "institutional cooking," its quantity causing us to ignore its quality).

The only reason I am here to minister to souls is that there are souls here to be ministered to—as is the case in any place where there are souls. The chief purpose for the existence of this institution is, however, not quite the same as *my* chief purpose.

"The purpose of this Institution," according to its own official pronouncement, "is to provide for such individuals, as nearly as possible, the kind of care, training, affection, encouragement and personal attention which they would receive in their own homes."

"Such individuals" is explained in the paragraph which precedes the statement quoted above: "The many hundreds of patients who make their home here are afflicted with mental retardation, which is simply arrested or imperfect intellectual development that prevents the mind from reaching an adult level." It does not prevent the soul from reaching the level of Heaven, however.

So I arrived—but just for a preliminary look. It was a sweltering day in June. Even without the aid of the weather, the mere prospect had made me hot under the collar. And under a Roman collar, that can be hot indeed. You could rightly say that my arrival was attended more by perspiration than inspiration.

Oh, I had seen institutions before—dimly. I had even met a retarded child or two—casually. I had heard about this place, too—vaguely. But here I am—actually! I, a plain ordinary clergyman, accustomed to dealing with plain, ordinary people in a plain, ordinary parish. And all of a sudden I am jolted out of my plain, ordinary little world and catapulted into—into—

Well, that is just it—into what? For all I know, a dark, sinister, uncharted, unkind, bleak, depressing, eerie, weird, disagreeable, subhuman, subnormal, sub—

Red, amber, green. That means "go." Turn this corner, go up the hill, and you will then have entered that world —dark, sinister, uncharted. . . .

There it is. That must be the Administration Building. "Keep to the left," he said. "Follow the road around." Around? Around which way? There are roads curving in every direction. "Then you will come to a building." A building? There are hundreds of buildings. Oh, yes, . . . "a building with a cross out by the curb." A cross, a cross, I have to look for a cross. That's what I am looking for—a cross.

There it is. His cross. *My* cross. Now where do I park? Around. That is what he said: "Around behind the building." Around. How appropriate! "Follow the road around. Park around—" My head is swimming. I am going around —in circles. Look at this place—the size of it! The number of buildings! And (worst of all) what is *inside* those buildings?

Whew! Am I hot!

II

ON THE MERRY-GO-ROUND

SITTING behind his desk behind the door of the building behind the cross, my predecessor was very cordial—and casual. Almost nonchalant. As though he had been introducing the place to one successor after another. But he was the *first* resident Chaplain here. And *I* might be the second. God, help me!

Every priest is accustomed to living with records, filing systems, and bookkeeping paraphernalia. But the items that my confrere spread on the desk before me that June day were anything but familiar: IQ lists, transfer cards, ward references, medical classifications, psychiatric evaluations, psychological results.

Then he started talking about the Director, the Chief Supervising Nurse, occupational therapy, psychometric examinations, community placement—and phenylketonuria. Wha-at?

Oh, what a hot day!

Finally, after what seemed to be an interminable dis-

16

cussion of technical matters, we stepped across the hall from the office. For the first time, I felt comfortable as we knelt in the tiny chapel and said a little prayer. I said the same one that had been pounding in my heart ever since my arrival: "God, help me!"—only more fervently.

Then we went upstairs—to the living quarters. I had lived in a house, a room, a rectory. Somehow, when I heard that term "living quarters," the reality hit me. I am going to "live" in an institution. This is where I will be "quartered." Suddenly I felt like a martyr.

"Nice quarters," I said very calmly, "for an institution. Where does *that* doorway go?"

"Oh, that leads to the rest of the building—forty patients over there."

Patients? Under the same roof? Forty of them?

"Who," I ventured, "cooks your meals?"

"Oh, I do."

You do! No cook? No housekeeper?

Noticing the dismay reflected on my face, my friend attempted to offer some consolation: "I have a male patient working for me. He's a big help."

A patient! I'll bet he's a big help. A patient. One of my parishioners. My parishioners from now on will be patients. I wonder: "How many are there here, anyhow?"

"Thirty-nine hundred," he said without the slightest trace of emotion.

Thir-ty-nine hun-dred! Patients? Thirty-nine hundred *patients?*

He saw the astonishment on my face again and once more offered consolation: "But only sixteen hundred of them are yours."

Is that all? Only sixteen hundred? Sixteen *hundred!*

"Shall we take a jaunt around the grounds?" he was saying.

A jaunt, he said. That is what I mean when I say he was almost nonchalant.

"Sure," I said, trying to sound as though I meant that I could hardly wait.

I should have, though. I should have waited. It really was not fair to the place. Physically I was completely wilted. My Roman collar felt as though it had been soaked in the Trevi Fountain. Mentally, I was thoroughly bewildered, and emotionally, I was splintered, as though my heart had been hit by a pile driver.

No, it really was not the time to take a jaunt around the grounds. But that was what I had come for, after all: to see the place.

"You haven't seen anything yet." He was comforting again. How casually he anticipated my every fear!

We drove in his little foreign car. It seemed so little in this big place, next to these big buildings, flitting from one to the other, like the fly not missing a chocolate in the box—but no more foreign than everything else I was seeing that day.

I had never seen so many buildings. Bricks, bricks, bricks, bricks. I am sure that if they were laid end to end, they would go around the earth several times. But they were not laid end to end. They were piled row on row on row—to what seemed to be dizzying heights—with mortar in between, tons and tons and tons of mortar. And windows—enough glass to put the entire African jungle into a greenhouse.

18

Every building had a name. Like the elevator operator in a department store, my escort reeled them off as we passed by, together with the type of facility and the category of patient which each one housed. I heard him, just as you hear the elevator operator. He sounds very helpful when you know what you want and what floor it is on. The difference was that I did not know. I had no idea of where I was going to get off. He told me: "Let's drop in here. You can see what a ward is like."

A ward! Another inanimate object. Like a ton of those bricks I had been thinking about stringing around the world, it struck me that the only person I had seen so far was my nonchalant friend. It was lunchtime. The patients were all indoors. And that is where we were going now—indoors, where the patients were! The pile driver came down on my heart with another splintering thump.

"This is a dayroom. They should be coming in from lunch now."

They did. They came. *From* lunch? *With* lunch, it seemed—so many of them had drooled, dribbled, and dripped. My companion anticipated my question again: "These are severely retarded boys. They are able to feed themselves only with difficulty. The attendants will get them all cleaned up now."

Severely retarded. The poor kids! No wonder my "Hello" did not get through to them. Retarded. You can see it. They look retarded. But that isn't all: so many of them! He spoke my thoughts again: "Many of them are physically handicapped, too. But the really deformed ones are in here. This is the back dormitory."

Oh, no! The shock flashed to my face.

19

"You'll get used to it."

Used to it? Now, look here, this nonchalance has gone a little too far. Who can "get used" to hydrocephalics, spastics, cretins, mongoloids? *I* did not know these terms; he was reeling them off again. I was just reeling.

And wilting. The heat had not lessened. And what I was seeing did not tend to bring my temperature down. But it was not only what I was seeing. You can hear the severely retarded, too, but you cannot understand what you hear. And on a hot day the odor is bound to be bad when— He was saying it: "So many are incontinent. They have a lot of laundry here."

My guide even pointed nonchalantly. He was pointing at a veritable mountain of bags filled with soiled laundry —as though it happened everyday.

But it *does* happen everyday. All of this. It all happens everyday, and I may be here to see it happening everyday. This may soon be *my* domain. Oh-h-h . . .

"I thought it would be best to show you the worst first. This next ward is quite different."

My escort was not only casual, but merciful—and shrewd. We were in the little foreign car again, spinning around through the winding roadways. It seemed a symbol to me, that little foreign car spinning around—a symbol of the strange merry-go-round I was on.

More than ever I felt that way now. There were patients all over: some running and shouting in play areas; some marching in front of an attendant; others sitting or walking in ones, twos, and threes. And from every direction, shouts of "Hi, Father!" "Hello, Father!" "Who's that, Father?" "Look at the other Father!"

The confusion made me dizzy, but through the haze of my amazement, a new perception was dawning. My friend's words crystallized it for me again.

"You see, these kids are more like the ones you've been accustomed to. They're only mildly or moderately retarded."

Only? Well, it was a great relief after those we had seen on the ward. But now he almost seemed cruel—not just nonchalant. Imagine saying, "He's *only* blind in *one* eye," or "She's *only* missing *one* leg." How awful!

We were entering the ward that was to be "quite different." It was. The first had been a boy's ward. These were girls.

"Class girls," he said.

That was all. That was all I heard—from him. He was mobbed. He must have felt like a teen-agers' television idol —squeals and all. Above the turmoil I could hear requests for rosaries and medals and remarks that sounded like, "Will you write my mother a letter," "Yesterday was my birthday," "I'm going home tomorrow," and "Cindy hit me."

Then it hit *me!* My friend's fan club shifted its focal point. Now I was being barraged: "Who are you?" "Are you a Father?" "Did you bring us something?" "What's your name?" "Are you his brother?" "You're big!"

Somewhere out of the tumult a merciful attendant rescued us by deciding it was time for the girls to line up for class. They did. Quietly and quickly. Order out of chaos— almost like a military academy. And away they marched, in front of the attendant.

My guide introduced me to the "Charge." She was very

motherly when she talked about her girls. As she showed us through her building, I seemed to have alighted from the merry-go-round for the first time. There were only a few working girls left on the ward. I noticed that they were a little older and perhaps a little—duller, more retarded than the others.

"They do the housework," the Charge was explaining.

Housework. Yes, it does look like a house—in a way.

"We try to make it as homelike as possible," she added.

Homelike? It *is* their home, isn't it? Well, I guess if you stretched your imagination far enough, you could imagine a family with sixty-nine children. That is what it added up to.

"There are thirty-nine beds in this dorm and thirty in the one across the hall."

Dorm. If it's a home, why can't they say "bedroom"? And "living room" instead of "dayroom"? Well, at least they do not eat in a "refectory."

"This is the dining room."

More working girls. Mopping, washing, wiping. They certainly keep the place clean. Colorful draperies. And flowers—in little wall pockets. I have not seen any of those in years. It's really cheerful in here. Kind of homelike. The woman's touch is evident in so many ways. Yes, this ward is "quite different." It was good to be off the merry-go-round.

"Well, Father, shall we continue our jaunt?"

Back on the carousel again. Well, the respite was nice while it lasted. I showed my appreciation in glowing words of gratitude to the Charge.

"It was a pleasure, Father. We'll be looking forward to working with you."

Working with me? That's right—they don't know. They think the appointment is final. To them, I *am* the new Chaplain of this place. *Mama mia!*

III

LIFE IN THE LIVING QUARTERS

"GOOD-MORNING," he said as I stepped into the dining room after my Mass. It was the voice of my pastor—back in the parish where I was still a curate.

"Good-morning."

I must have groaned, because he looked a little concerned when he asked, "Don't you feel well this morning?"

"Oh, yes," I managed. "Just a little tired, didn't sleep too well last night."

"Well, you'll feel better after a little breakfast." He smiled as he left to go up to his room.

"Sure," I said, adding under my breath, "All I need is a little breakfast. If only he knew!"

But he did not. He did not know that I was the lucky fellow who had been out to look over the job at the State School yesterday. He did not know that I would have to call the Bishop in a few minutes and tell him what I thought.

What I thought? How could I tell the Bishop what I

thought? How can you think after an experience like that? Oh, I had thought—all night. But all the thoughts of the night had added up to just one thing: a nightmare. And it had not stopped. It was still a nightmare—right in broad daylight. It had kept me from sleeping. Now it was keeping me from eating.

After explaining to the cook that I just was not hungry —and how could she understand that, with the appetite I always had?—I, too, went up to my room. My room—in the rectory. Not my "living quarters" in a huge brick building. With the pastor on the other side of the wall—not forty patients. Lord, help me! What do I say to the Bishop?

What could I say? I did not know. So that is what I said: "I just don't know, Bishop. I just don't know."

I had never had a choice in any of my previous assignments. Few of us do. But when it came to these specialized jobs, it was different. Now I was being given a choice, and all I could say was, "I don't know."

But the Bishop knew. He knew he wanted me as Chaplain at the State School. I could still decline the offer. Offer? It seemed a sentence. Still, I was flattered to think that the Bishop deemed me capable.

"I'm not, though," I was saying. "I'm not capable. I haven't had any special training. That's what the Director of the State School asked me yesterday, if I had any special training. And I haven't."

"But you have," said His Excellency. "You've had seminary training—and seventeen years in the priesthood."

"But clinical training. I haven't had an ounce of it."

"You'll get tons of it, right there on the job. I think you can do it."

"I don't know." There it was again. I felt so stupid. It's a good thing the Bishop is a kind and patient man, I thought. But he has to know. I have to give him an answer —now.

"Well, take another day or two. Go down again tomorrow. Look it over a little more. Give it a little more thought —and prayer. But call me the first thing Thursday morning. I'll have to know your decision by then without fail."

"Thank you, Bishop." Thank you, thank you! That is what I need, another look, a little thought. And prayer—a lot of prayer.

So I had another look. I thought—my head off. And I prayed—my heart out. And Thursday morning I was back on the phone, talking to the Bishop.

"I just don't know, Bishop. I just don't know." That would have been enough for a less astute man, but not for this Bishop. He wanted to know why I didn't know. So I told him all the reasons why I didn't know why I didn't know. And he patiently considered them, one by one. And then he left the choice up to me. So I made my choice.

"You are my superior," I said. "God's will is expressed through you. If you want me to go, I'll go."

"I do," he said gently, but with conviction.

And that was just how I felt: gently convicted.

One week later the official document of my appointment as Chaplain of the State School arrived in the morning mail. Everyone was astonished—except for me. *I* was numb —for the tenth day in a row.

I was numb while I packed my belongings, while I prepared my farewell sermon to the parish, even when I preached it. When I got behind the wheel of my car and headed east, I was still numb.

And so I arrived, bag and baggage, numb and dumb, at my living quarters. Not just for a look this time, but for good. Good? So many times, I had asked others to repeat after me, "For better or for worse." Which would this prove to be? "Oh, dear God, please let it be for better. Better for these patients, better for me, better for—better for whatever You want it to be better for," I was saying as I knelt in the tiny chapel—*my* chapel.

It was cluttered now. The little truck with my major belongings had arrived ahead of me, and they were scattered everywhere, including the chapel. My predecessor had already moved out, leaving blank spaces here and there. My things were now occupying the blank spaces.

I suppose the upstairs is a mess, too. Well, excuse me, Lord, I had better get busy. I shall have to get this chapel straightened out for Mass in the morning. But I had better see what the upstairs is like first.

"Welcome to your new home! I'm Emma. You won't understand my last name for a while, so just call me Emma." She was cleaning out the refrigerator. A man was scrubbing the kitchen floor. I recognized him as my predecessor's houseboy, a patient by the name of Ted. But I had never laid eyes on Emma before. She was "just an old friend" of the former Chaplain, she told me, and thought she ought to get the place cleaned up a little.

She had. Everything was spick-and-span. She showed me where she had already hung my clothes and where she had put the suitcases that had come in the truck. She pointed out the things she had left in the refrigerator for my lunch and told me how to get to her house for supper. And with a "Now, I'll get out of your way," she was gone.

I was not quite so numb any more. It is strange how a friendly person can bring you to life. I was looking after her down the stairway, not so numb, but still pretty dumb —or dumbfounded. I had not said much to Emma—she had taken me so by surprise.

Ted had finished scrubbing the floor and was asking me what I wanted him to do now. I did not know. I did not know where to begin. And I did not know Ted. For Ted was a patient. What could I expect a retarded child to do? Child? Ted was a year older than I was. He looked like a banker—even when he was scrubbing the floor. He was smoking a cigarette. He spoke clearly and sensibly. He was friendly. He really did not seem much different from other people I had known.

He is not. He is not much different. He looks and acts like—like a lot of people. I do not know what I expected. I guess I expected him to be different—more different. Well, I might as well find out what he can do.

"Will you bring in the things from the trunk of my car? Do you know what a Rambler looks like?"

"Sure, Father. What's your license number?"

Can he *read?*

"Sure, I can read. I read all about you in yesterday's paper."

He reads the *newspaper?* And what is he doing with the pencil?

"I'll write down the number of your car, so I'm sure I get the right one."

He *writes!*

"May I have the keys, please?"

Keys! Can I trust him?

"It's all right, Father. I don't know how to drive."

He reads *minds!*

"Should I bring everything in out of the trunk?"

The spare tire?

"I mean, all the luggage?"

"Yes, please."

What else does he know? Maybe he's one of those idiot savants. Maybe he *can* read my mind. Oh, how ridiculous! I should have told him to bring my Breviary off the front seat. No, he certainly wouldn't know what a Breviary is. I would have to say "prayer book."

"Here's the luggage, Father. And I brought your prayer book off the front seat, too."

Oh, no!

"Should I go up after the mail now? I didn't get it this morning."

Is it safe? Can he read the mail without opening it? Now, stop that! Yes, Ted, do get the mail—so I can get my thoughts settled.

"I'll be right back. Then I'll help you get settled."

What in the world is he doing in this institution? He's *retarded?* The file cards—that's it. I'll look at his card while he's gone; that will tell me his IQ—and maybe more. Downstairs in the office. Let's see, now, those files were at the left of the desk. Ah, here they are. Ted . . . Ted . . . but I don't know his name!

Well, I later learned his name, and his IQ, and his background, as I was eventually to learn the names and the IQ's and the backgrounds of hundreds of these patients;

but I had already learned the most important fact about these people from the first retarded person I ever really knew, my houseboy, Ted.

He *is* retarded. And he is *not* an idiot savant. He cannot read minds—or letters through their envelopes. He can read and write and do a lot of other things, but he needs constant supervision. Many things he cannot do. Others he can do only slowly or poorly. Some things he does very well. But he could never organize his life and conduct his affairs on his own. The development of his mental ability has been arrested, and it will never reach the normal level. Otherwise, he is just like you and me. I learned that from him.

I was to learn much more from this retardate, too. As I took up my new life, it developed that this houseboy was also Mass server, errand boy, housekeeper, dishwasher, guide, and fact finder.

After he returned with the mail, Ted helped me "get settled." If he but knew how unsettled I really was! But he treated me as though I were in complete mastery of the situation. He knew where everything was and how a lot of things were done. But he did not tell me unless I asked. And he constantly asked me what I wanted and how I wanted it. He was making me aware of something. Gradually it dawned on me: I am the boss in this house.

And it *is* a house. Emma had even called it my "new home." It does not *have* to be called my "living quarters" just because it is in an institution. As Ted and I got things organized and my own familiar little belongings started to appear out of the bags and boxes, the place even began to *feel* like home.

After the chapel had been cleaned out, I realized what a pretty little place it was. And I thought, "This is God's house. He lives here and so do I. Even though my quarters are upstairs and His are down, we live under the same roof, God and I. I'm the boss. He's the Master."

It seemed no time at all before Ted and I had everything in order. Ted went back to his ward, and I went to Emma's house for supper. I met her husband, Achiel, and they both treated me like an old friend.

As I fell asleep in my new bed that night, weary and still bewildered, I was grateful that the presence of God and people like Emma and Achiel—and Ted—made me feel at home.

IV

ALL I SURVEY

TRYING to rub the disbelief out of my eyes, I was beginning my first full day as Chaplain by staring out of my bedroom window.

It is beautiful—just like a park. My front yard is just like a park: a lovely expanse of lawn, dotted with a variety of trees and shrubs, extending the two or three hundred feet out to the roadway, which curves gracefully around the front of the building. I hadn't seen it before. In my bewilderment and numbness the beauty of the landscape had escaped me. How could I have missed it?

Beyond the roadway, I saw an even greater source of wonderment. Two huge swimming pools. For the retarded? Swimming pools twenty to thirty feet deep—and no shallow end? No wonder they are securely fenced in. No wonder the bottoms of them are grown full of weeds. And the way they are constructed—all four cement sides slanting severely toward the center. Oh well, just another dream of some fanatic gone wild, I suppose. Just another wad of the taxpayers' money gone down the drain.

As my gaze wandered back across the road, I was struck by the serenity of the scene which lay before me. My "park" was so well kept. Right below the window a huge catalpa tree was just bursting into bloom. A light breeze wafted the fragrance of sweet syringa through the room. The picture was unmarred by traffic. The only sound was the song of birds as they flitted from tree to tree. My ears were as unbelieving as my eyes. The whole place had seemed so noisy and chaotic during my visits of inspection. And now, on this first morning, it all seemed so tranquil.

But I have to cease this reverie. Ted will be here at 6:45, and I have to let him in. I wonder if he will be on time.

He was—waiting on the porch when I unlocked the door at 6:30.

"Good-morning, Father." My disbelief returned. There he stood—looking like a banker—wearing a neat gray suit and a striped tie. Somehow his square jaw, speckled gray hair, and steel-rimmed glasses gave him an executive appearance. One thing about him that struck me was the immobility of his lips. He spoke clearly enough, but his lips moved only slightly. In fact, his face was usually quite expressionless. He did laugh and smile on occasion, but more often remained rather sphinxlike.

Although I smiled when I let him in that first morning, both of us were preoccupied with unraveling the mystery of our mutual new acquaintance. Ted went right to the sacristy to put on his cassock, while I knelt at the little altar railing. It would be the first time I had ever celebrated Mass right in my own house.

It was also the first time I had been served by a retarded altar boy. Ted did not know the longer Latin prayers, but he amazed me with the quality of his shorter responses. And he served the entire Mass without a mistake The congregation that morning was different from that which I had been accustomed to. It consisted of one white-uniformed nurse.

While I finished my prayers after Mass, Ted divested himself of his role as altar boy and went upstairs to assume his duties as housekeeper. By the time I arrived in the kitchen, the coffee had been brewed, the bed made, and the table set.

During breakfast I learned more about my houseboy. He had been in the service. His home was Buffalo. His father lived there alone now. But why was he here? That question remained unanswered, because it remained unasked.

After breakfast, without as much as a hint on my part, Ted started washing the dishes and announced that he would pick up the mail at 9:30 if I wanted him to. I did, but I also wanted to know where.

"At the Front. We have our own post office there." He explained that the Front was the Administration Building; this, I admitted to myself, was a handy way of expressing it.

Probably because it was the only place in my new working area which I could find, I decided to begin the minute exploration of my new job in the office. The whereabouts of various records and the contents of a variety of file drawers had been indicated to me by the former Chaplain, but I had not been very receptive at the time. Now that the first shock had worn off, perhaps I should become acquainted with some of the paraphernalia which he had revealed to my bewildered mind at the time of my first visit.

Most offices are rather similar in appearance. This one is no exception. There is the desk with the usual letter baskets, pen, ink, stapler, paperweight, calendar pad, and gooseneck lamp. There are the usual filing drawers, a steel storage cabinet, reference books, a couple of chairs, a typewriter, and two telephones—the state phone and my own private one.

None of these things is arranged to my taste, of course, but the stamp of my personality can wait. Right now I have to delve under appearances. The desk seems to be the logical place to begin. And that requires a key.

Key? Look at them—dozens of keys. I'm sure the ring they are on is the hoop from a nail keg. And I don't recognize a single one of them. Let's see, is that the one Ted used for the sacristy cupboard this morning? Ted—that's it; maybe he knows the desk key.

He does. And so my retarded friend solves another mystery for me. Mystery? This desk is full of them. The center drawer is commonplace enough: paper clips and paper paste, rubber bands and rubber stamps, typing ribbon and postage stamps, tape, string, lighter fluid, ink eradicator—and keys. Apparently one key ring is not big enough.

The contents of the bottom drawers are also very ordinary. But take a look inside these top ones! Both are filled with file folders, all neatly labeled. And look at the labels: "Admissions Chronologically," "Boarding Home Patients," "Colonies," "Department Heads' Meetings," "Estimate Requests," "Interdisciplinary Conference," "Mongoloid Characteristics," "Rehabilitation Facilities," "Requisitions." Not a single subject I have ever dealt with before. Well, maybe the books will be more familiar.

They are—as familiar as the file folders! I recognize them as books. But their titles are just as strange: *Facilities for Exceptional Children, Department Policy Manual, Report of the Board of Visitors, A.A.M.D. Directory, A.M.H.C. Report,* and so on and on.

Obviously, I have a lot of reading to do. I know the little file drawers will not be any more encouraging. They contain the patients' index and transfer cards, with all sorts of mysterious information. They will require some detailed study, too.

"Anything to go up Front, Father?" It was Ted, on his way to get the mail. "Up Front" still sounded strange, but I remembered that it was the abbreviation for the Administration Building. Therefore, Ted tells me, "anything to go up Front" could be mail for the post office, requisitions for the business office, "will-calls" for the switchboard, work for my secretary (in the medical office), communications to the Director—or anyone else within a mile radius. Despite the broad choice, I was unable to produce a single item that needed to go up Front.

But Ted went up Front. It is a good thing, because I could never find my way—up or back down. And that reminds me: when Ted gets back, I had better make a little circuit of the grounds. I guess I can find my way around the office, now, even though most of its contents still mystify me. And the sooner I start to find my way around the rest of my parish, the better. I might get a sick call and—

The phone! Which one? Dial tone. It must be the other, the state phone.

"Hello."

"Chaplain?"

"Yes."

"The doctor just put Jerome Loughlin on the critical list. Can you come down, please?"

"Yes. Where?"

"On BH3."

"Where is that?"

"Boys' Hospital."

"How do I get there?"

"Just cross East Maple, go around the circle in front of the West Dorm, follow the road between the Service Building and the East Dorm, around behind the South Dorm, and you'll be right in front of the Boys' Hospital."

"Thank you. I'll be right there."

What a rash promise! I don't know the East Dorm from the West or the back of the South Dorm from the front of the Boys' Hospital. Now what do I do? Better start with the map. Ah, here it is. Hospital. Boys' Hospital. Is this a map or a Chinese puzzle? Buildings, but no names. Well, here I go.

Wait a minute—what do I need? Ritual, stole, oils, pyx— But can he receive Communion? I didn't ask. How old is he? Is he nauseated? He is retarded. Has he *made* his First Communion? Is he capable of being anointed? The card. His index card. Loughlin, Jerome. Jerome Loughlin. Born: 1930. IQ: 20. MA (mental age): 2-10. Baptized: blank. Not baptized. Severely retarded. Baptism. That's all. Just baptize him. Baptismal water. I don't have any. Where's the holy water? In the jug—the jug in the sacristy.

It's labeled "holy water." Hurry. Cotton. Stole. Holy water.

I wish they would move this building a little closer to my parking space. I may as well walk all the way. No. The car is faster if I get lost. Let's see: Cuyler; that's Maple. Cross it. This must be the circle. Around to the road between the buildings. There it is. Now right—past the Service Building. That must be the Service Building. South Dorm. Is that the South Dorm? Behind it, she said. Where is the *front* of it? Oh, oh, another circle. This must be the back. That's it; that's the Boys' Hospital. A sign. There's a sign: HOSPITAL. It just says HOSPITAL. *Boys'* Hospital?

"That's it, Father. That's the Boys' Hospital."

"Thank you. Thanks a lot."

How did he know I was looking for the Boys' Hospital? What a building! Where do I go now? There's an office. I'll ask.

"Right straight through to the elevator, Father, for BH3."

I didn't have to ask. Which way on the elevator?

"Up, Father, for BH3. Turn right when you get off. The office is down at the end, to the left."

"Thank you."

Everybody has been posted. They knew I would get lost.

"Hello, Father. Jerome's in a side room. Follow me, please. He's had pleurisy, and it's gone into pneumonia. The doctor doesn't think he'll make it. Anything I can do?"

"I'm going to baptize him. We'll need a sponsor."

"I'm a Catholic, Father. I'll be glad to do it. Here's our

38

Jerome. Poor fellow! He's so spastic, and now his breathing is so difficult."

"Does he understand?"

"Not a thing. Never has spoken a word. I used to know him when I worked on Infirmary Two. No one ever came to see him."

"No?"

"Not a soul. Just abandoned, I guess."

"Maybe that's why we have no record of Baptism for him. Well, we'll see that he's a child of God anyhow. *Si tu non es baptizatus, Hieronyme, ego te baptizo in nomine Patris, et Filii, et Spiritus Sancti.* There we are, my boy; now you're all ready for Heaven."

"Isn't it wonderful, Father? He can't miss, can he?"

"That's right—unimpeded passage. Do you just have sick patients on this ward, Miss—"

"Evelyn Armstrong, Father. Oh, my, no. The new admission ward is here, pediatrics, isolation, and the little boys."

"Little boys?"

"Yes. We have seventy severely retarded boys under ten."

"All here?"

"All here. After you sign the sick-call book, I'll show you my darlings."

Darlings? *Her* darlings? That is what she said. And she meant it. I could see that when she took me into the two dayrooms. She knew them all by name—even though they did not know their own. And they flocked around her like a swarm of bees. Many of them seemed to understand her, even though none of them could speak more than a word

39

or two. But somehow they were communicating with her, and she with them. I decided it was the language of love.

Standing unnoticed at the door of the first dayroom, I wondered how they would respond to me. Will they scream and run away? Or will they stand up to me and fight? Well, I may as well find out. How do you talk to little boys who don't know how to talk back? What can you say to someone who can't undersand anything? Listen to *her*. Miss Armstrong is doing it—just as naturally as can be—talking and smiling. All I have to do is the same thing.

"Hello, boys," I ventured, "how are you today?" I was forcing a big smile.

That was all that was necessary. Now we all are friends. Not one of them is screaming or running away or kicking me. They're just inspecting me. For sheer size, some of them have probably never seen the like of me. But they are not afraid. In fact, many of them are smiling, even hanging onto me and reaching to be picked up. Just like other little boys. They want to be loved. They need a mother, like Miss Armstrong. And a father, like—

Leaving the Boys' Hospital, I was overwhelmed with but one thought. I had just given spiritual birth to Jerome Loughlin. He apparently had been abandoned by his parents. All these children are away from their families. They are children. They must hunger for love and affection just as all children do. Who gives it to them day after day? I had seen: people like Miss Armstrong. *I* have to be one of those people. When those who can talk call me Father, they have to mean it, and the rest of them have to believe it, even if they cannot say it.

As I got into the car, this thought was given emphasis

on every side. There were shouts of greeting from all directions. How different from what I had been accustomed to! Nobody greets you as you walk down the city street unless he is acquainted with you. But here everybody passes the time of day. What a nice custom!

Getting back to the Moss Building, where I live, from the Boys' Hospital is really a simple matter—if you know their relative positions. That morning it was obvious that I did not. Oh, well, I had intended to take a jaunt around the grounds anyway.

I wonder what that building is. It looks newer than the rest, and it looks as if it is the last one in this direction. Let's see; this road should get me back. That's a big sports field. I wonder how many of them are able to use it. Nobody out there now. They must like to swing. Swings all over the place. East Maple Avenue. That's the dividing line. I remember that. Boys on one side; girls on the other. My building must be on the right. Now where *is* it? I must have to turn here.

Just look at those buildings! One right after the other. And not one of them looks like the Moss. This must be the Girls' Division, though. Not a boy in sight. Plenty of girls. Wonder if they're all patients. They must be—they're all waving and shouting "Hello."

That must be the Front. It looks like one of those hotels in Saratoga Springs. What a view from here! I didn't realize this place was so high. You can see the whole countryside. I suppose the village is down that way. I had better not get mixed up with that today.

Suddenly I remembered Ted—and the mail—and the operator. I had forgotten to tell the operator where I was going. And I had not brought my keys along. The two things my predecessor said I should always be sure to do: "Always take your keys with you, and let the operator know where you'll be." And I didn't do either one of them. And I'm lost. I haven't the slightest idea where my place is.

Thank the Lord—there's a patrolman. He'll tell me how to get back. I'll just pull up beside him.

"Good morning, Father. I'm Jim Meath. You must be the new Chaplain—you look lost."

"I am—both. And I'm doubly pleased to meet you. I'm sure you know your way around here."

"I do, Father—now. But I used to get lost, too. Everybody does. Where are you headed for?"

"That's the funny part of it: home. I don't even know where I live."

"That's a good one, Father. Just follow me. I'll show you the way. That's what we're here for. Anytime you need any help, just give us a call."

"Thanks, Jim. I'll try to stay close behind you."

"It's not very far. Just around that bend. I'll toot my horn when we get there. See you later, Father."

What a nice fellow! Everyone is so accommodating. I wonder if these policemen have much violence to contend with. Violence? I'd never thought of that! And I'd better not—at least till I can find my way around this place.

There it is—the Moss Building. Why, I must have gone right by it on my way toward the Front. Now, I hope I can keep track of it while I'm finding that parking lot. Let's see; three left-hand turns should do it. East Maple. Cuyler. That's it. I guess I know the way from here. Wonder why they don't have better access to that building.

Well, at least I'll get my daily walk in. It *would* be nice if I had a garage, though.

I suppose Ted is wondering what happened to me. Maybe he gave up and went back to the ward—or fell asleep.

"Hi, Father."

"Well, Ted, what in the world—"

"Oh, I thought I'd get this porch mopped while I was waitin'. It's pretty dirty. The phone's been ringin', but I didn't answer it—not s'posed to."

"That's my fault. I forgot to tell the operator where I was going. I had a sick call and left in a hurry."

"Your mail's on the desk, Father. Not much today."

"OK, Ted. Thanks."

Not much? Look at that stack! But it's not really *mail*. Memo from the business office. Recreation schedule. *Civil Service Leader*. Oh, yes, here's a letter. New admission card. Transfer sheet. Psychometric test—review. Another letter. Department heads' meeting notice. Estimate request forms. *Policy Manual* inserts.

I am lost again. This is worse than trying to find my way around the grounds. Oh, if only something *normal* would happen!

It did. I opened one of the two real letters in my mail and found that it was a bill—the telephone bill for last month. And I hadn't even made a call yet. But at least it's something I recognize. Familiar items are heartwarming in a strange land—even if they happen to be distasteful things.

On the other hand, look at this other letter, addressed to the Catholic Chaplain, from a Mrs. Saginowski. She's a

43

social worker for the Ontario County Department of Public Welfare, and she wants to know at what age a child with an IQ of 50 should be permitted to make his First Communion and what course of instruction I would suggest.

I have prepared scores of children for their first Communion, but I never knew the IQ of a single one of them. I have used all kinds of instruction material, but none of it was ever intended for retarded children.

I certainly have a lot to learn. The only things I recognize in this desk are the paper clips and rubber bands. I can't even find my way home. The only part of my mail that means anything to me is a telephone bill—which isn't even mine.

It is only noon of my first day here. I have certainly seen plenty in half a day. And I have arrived at one definite conclusion: I am not master of all I survey.

V

"I LIKE YOU"

THREE days had elapsed since my arrival. Ted had been here for five years and consequently could identify all the buildings and many of the personnel. Most of the three days amounted to an almost continual roll call. From the front porch, my houseboy recited over and over for me the names of all the buildings that could be seen from that vantage point. They did not amount to even half of the total of sixty-five, but at least I was becoming familiar with my immediate surroundings.

For some reason or other, I had assumed that all the buildings were occupied by patients. In a city, however, you find not only residences, but also establishments for the myriad services that the homes and their inhabitants require. And this place is a little city. So, besides the patients' dwellings, I can see from my porch such places as the Powerhouse, the Service Building, and the Storehouse.

The Kane Home and the Armstrong are also nearby.

45

They are two of our three employees' apartment houses, Ted tells me. Members of the staff also occupy another building and several houses strung around the base of the hill, he says.

Staff, employees, patients, buildings, departments, services. Good heavens! How will I ever learn the names of all of them? Well, at least I know the Moss; the Burnham; the Female Infirmary; Cottages F, G, H, and I; and the East and West Dorms. Those are the patients' buildings that I can see from here. And what I have to know most of all is where to find the patients.

It should not have surprised me, I suppose, that more than a quarter of the institution's population is made up of employees. Another 1,000 names to learn! Oh, well, at least I do not have to know all 3,900 patients. Only 1,600 are mine. So far I had become acquainted with 2 of them, Jerome Loughlin and Ted. And Jerome had gone to his eternal reward this morning. As for employees, my percentage was better. I had met Jim Meath, Evelyn Armstrong, and, of course, the Director, Dr. Henne. Maybe I shall do better in the next three days. When I know the buildings, then I can start finding out who is in them. So far I have spent most of my time familiarizing myself with my own quarters, figuring that I can't run the bases if I don't know home plate.

The three rooms upstairs contain all the commonplace furnishings of a home, many of them my own possessions. All I have to get used to is their arrangement. The supplies and equipment in the sacristy and chapel are also the customary things.

The one room in the house that really stumped me was the office. So ordinary on the surface, it embraced untold secrets, many of which would become meaningful to me only little by little with the passage of time and the development of events.

Perhaps I would become enlightened as things started to happen. They were going to start the next morning, when sixty or seventy patients from four different wards would be coming to the chapel for Confession. This was the regular Saturday morning routine from nine to twelve o'clock.

They came. Every forty-five minutes a small group of girls thundered up the front steps, since the little chapel seats only twenty. With each group was an attendant, who checked off the names of the girls on her Communion list. This was necessary, I discovered, to assure that only those capable would come for Confession—and receive Communion the next day. It was my first practical lesson in the application of supervision, which is such an important element in the life of the retarded.

Since the chapel is so small, there is no space for a confessional. Therefore, I was hearing Confessions at a portable one in the office across the hall. It is not the usual place for administering the Sacrament, but I could not help feeling that it was the first thing of consequence I had done in that room. It also struck me that it was singularly appropriate that consciences should be unburdened in this chamber of secrets.

As each group of patients arrived, I made the acquaintance of another attendant. Then I would kneel with the girls in the chapel for a short prayer. I was astonished at their apparent devotion and at the utter silence while they were thinking of their sins.

One of my early determinations was that I must always remember that these patients were children. Not the least of the shocks I suffered during my first visit of inspection was the sight of so many physically old men and women. But they all had the minds and hearts of children. "I must remember that," I had said.

As difficult as it was to do, I did remember it that first Saturday morning. It happened that the wards scheduled for Confession that week were the A, B, and C Buildings and the Girls' Hospital. Most of these "girls" are above the age of twenty. Some of them are far above it. But they all are referred to as girls, and the old men are boys. The designation, which is, in fact, logical, helps me remember that every one of them is a child at heart, despite all appearances to the contrary.

That is the reason why I was so impressed with their behavior that day. I could well have expected some talking and laughing in the chapel while I was in the office. But there was not a sound. I might have attributed this unexpected deportment to the presence of the attendant, had I not, on many previous occasions, witnessed quite a different reaction from "normal" children—even while they were under the surveillance of nuns who were splendid disciplinarians.

Mildly and moderately retarded children who have sufficient mental ability to receive the Sacraments are one thing. The severely retarded, however, are another. The next day, there would be all kinds of them at Mass—old and young, weak and strong, boys and girls, speechless and talkative, calm and disturbed, and of almost every mental level *below* normal. Needless to say, it was the first time in my life I had ever been prepared for all hell to break loose in church.

Church. That is what the Assembly Hall is called on Sundays. On Saturday and Friday nights it is a movie house; on Wednesdays it is a dance hall; and in between, it serves as gym, conference chamber, banquet hall, and anything else for which a large gathering place is needed. Saturday mornings it is a synagogue for our Jewish patients, and on Sundays it alternates as a Catholic and Protestant church.

This situation increased my apprehension. It was aggravated even more when I visited the hall on Saturday afternoon. There were more than 500 folding chairs set up in a space that must have been intended for about 300. This left hardly room to sit. Kneeling would be out of the question.

A small stage was situated on one side of the Assembly Hall. At one end was a projection booth, and at the other a simple portable altar in front of two windows. Draperies of an unearthly green color had been drawn over the two windows, and a platform pushed up against the extra-long legs of the altar. In front of the platform stood a portable railing with kneeling bench.

That was the extent of my church, Ted informed me. No statues or pictures, no holy water fonts or baptismal font, no Stations of the Cross, no vigil lights—not even a collection basket. How could anyone summon up devotion in a place like that? I was convinced that pandemonium would reign supreme in the congregation I was expecting the next day.

I was wrong. As I entered the "sanctuary," the entire congregation rose respectfully. This I was accustomed to. When I started the prayers of the Mass, however, my devotion was disrupted—not by pandemonium—but by a loud chord sounded on a piano: it was our "church organ." And the chord was the signal for a choir of thirty or forty female patients to belt out a hymn. Since the choir was seated just to the right of the altar, I received full benefit of their offerings, which were rendered with uninhibited gusto. I was learning early that the retarded love to sing.

In contrast with the loudly sung praises of the choir girls, their first hymn was followed by absolute silence. It was so unusual—and so unexpected—that it disturbed me. It became a distraction: Had everyone else sneaked out under cover of that earsplitting melody? Or was it just the calm before the storm? No screams or shouts were being let loose. None of the metal chairs was being clanged. No feet were being shuffled. There was no talking or laughing—not even a whisper. Most surprising of all, there was not even the inevitable cough.

As I turned from the altar for the first *Dominus vobiscum,* I was relieved to see that everyone was still there. I then decided that it must certainly be the buildup. Perhaps they were so transfixed with this new personality standing at the altar that they were forgetting to misbehave. I concluded that the eruption would come as soon as the novelty of my appearance had worn off. After all, many of them had not even seen me before that morning. Most of them had not heard my voice.

That's it. They're waiting for the sermon. When I start to speak in English, that's when the chaos will begin. There's the first sound I've heard. They're rising for the reading of the Gospel. Well, at least they're still alive. Oh, Lord, help me keep my mind on my prayers!

After the Gospel was finished, everyone sat down. The announcements I had to make were very few. The time for the sermon had come.

The first sermon in a new assignment is usually not very doctrinal. I felt this was particularly fortuitous on this occasion, since I thoroughly doubted my ability to express the truths of Christianity on the retarded level. I was happy, therefore, to be able to begin my preaching to this congregation with a sort of acceptance speech.

I was saying how happy I was to be here. I was telling them that I wanted to be their friend, that I wanted to help them, and that I would do my best to be a good Chaplain to them. I was telling them that it would take us awhile to get acquainted and that I knew they would miss my predecessor. I said that I knew he liked them and was good to them, that they would miss him, because they also liked him. It was too bad he had to leave, I added, and I was sure that they felt very sorry, but—

Then it happened. Impatient with my lengthy belaboring of the point, one of the girls blurted out in a loud, clear voice, "We like you, too, Father Bauer!"

That was it. That was the eruption I had been expecting from the congregation—but totally unlike anything I could have expected. I have never discovered who the solitary speaker in the congregation was that first Sunday morning. I doubt that she had even laid eyes on me till then.

And I am sure she had not had time to gather any evidence that would evoke either love or hate for the new Chaplain. But it was the spontaneous expression of a trait that is outstanding and very common among the retarded: they *like* people. And it brought my sermon to a most fitting conclusion, since I had unwittingly hit on the words which these "children" wanted to hear above all others. Could anyone have responded otherwise? The magic expression simply leaped to my lips: "And *I* like *you!*"

VI

WE BECOME FRIENDS

THE voice of approval that rang out that Sunday morning was not only the first disturbance during church services. It was also the last. Now and then a patient subject to seizures may have a spell in church, but a deliberate disturbance is unheard of. As time went on, I discovered that retarded children behave well in other circumstances, too. This is not to say that none of them is ever naughty. Everyone gets off the track once in a while, and retardates are no exception.

The fact remains, however, that the group conduct of these people is absolutely astonishing. For three years some of my catechism classes embraced the ridiculous number of 200 patients. Yet discipline was never a problem. In the same hall where these patients worship God on Sunday, they attend a movie on Friday or Saturday. You would expect turmoil—especially when you realize how little of the picture many of them understand. Instead, you behold a quiet, orderly audience, apparently engrossed in every film they see.

But I was not aware of this phenomenon the first time I celebrated the Lord's Day with my new parishioners. This was not the only revelation made to me that day, nor was this the only day of revelation. The discoveries of that Sunday morning were only the beginnings of the many things I was destined to learn at this school.

The conversion of our Assembly Hall from movie house to Catholic church to Protestant church to dance hall is a major operation which occurs every week—sometimes more than once, if there is a holy day or some special service. Following that first Mass, I saw the operation take place. There were things happening which would start to acquaint me with some of those names I had to learn.

Out of the dispersing crowd emerged a woman by the name of Helen Banckert. She is the staff attendant in the A Building. On alternate Sundays (and whenever else she is on duty) she is in charge of the hall. Her assistant, Mrs. Hawk, does the same stint when Mrs. Banckert is away. Two of their girls, patients in the A Building, are my sacristans, I discovered. Under the direction of Mrs. Banckert or Mrs. Hawk, Sarah and Janet set up and take down. That means that they get everything ready for church services and undo after the service whatever they did before. This sometimes entails mopping the floor and setting up or taking down more than 500 folding chairs. But no matter how much work is involved, the Assembly Hall never fails to become a church whenever it is needed.

When evening devotions are held, the operation is in charge of another A Building attendant by the name of Mrs. Kirckpatrick. But day or night, Sarah and Janet are always on the job. Overseeing the whole program of As-

sembly Hall conversion is one of the female area supervisors, Mrs. Manley. She tells me that she has been taking
care of the innumerable details involved in such things as
First Communion and Confirmation ceremonies for many
years and that she is prepared to continue in that capacity.

Mrs. Manley happens to be a Catholic. None of the
other ladies is. But I was not long in deciding that they
all are pillars of the church. No detail is too small to elicit
their scrupulous attention, so that church will be as edify-
ing as possible for the patients, whether Catholic, Protestant, or Jewish.

In fact, I am convinced that the ecumenical movement
was in operation in institutions long before it began to develop in society at large. Circumstances have made it a
practical necessity. The other resident Chaplain, realizing
this fact (which I had yet to learn), had already dropped
in to introduce himself. An affable fellow by the name of
Blaisdell, he pledged himself to cooperate in every way
possible. From the very start he made me feel at ease with
Protestantism and at home with the Chaplaincy.

Not only was I new to the Chaplaincy, I learned, but
the Chaplaincy was also new to the State School. Full-time
Chaplains had been provided for the Department of Mental Hygiene only five years before my arrival. Previously,
the spiritual needs of the patients in these institutions
were provided for by the neighboring clergy. It could be
expected, then, that the constant presence of clergymen
on the grounds might be overlooked or ignored by members of the staff who, for years on end, had been accustomed to calling a minister or priest only in emergencies.

It was a pleasant surprise, therefore, when the phone

in my office rang the day after that first Sunday and the caller said, "I am not a Catholic, but one of your girls on my ward is very disturbed. I think it would be good if she could go to Confession." A few days later another attendant called to say that Joe Murdock had gotten into trouble and that he would like to bring him over for some counseling.

My new assignment was only a week old, but many of my early misgivings had already been dispelled. I still did not know my way around very well, in more ways than one. I was sure of the location of only 3 or 4 of the 31 wards and just a handful of the 65 buildings. Of my 1,600 patients and the 1,000 employees, I knew the names of about a dozen each.

But I had already learned some startling things—about the employees, the patients, the buildings, the wards, and the whole place in general. Perhaps the two most essential facts that were impressed on me that first week were that I had absolutely nothing to fear, but a lot to learn. And I saw that these two elements were strangely related. I would not have to worry about all I had to learn, because I was surrounded by countless experienced and capable people who would help me to learn it, to say nothing of patients like Ted and Sarah and Janet, who were teaching me fast. And, of course, it was for practically the same reasons that I had nothing to fear. I do not know why I should have expected otherwise, but one thought came as a revelation to me, nevertheless (and it summarizes all the discoveries of that first week): I suddenly realized that I was among friends.

VII

THE BATTLEFIELD

BASICALLY, the Chaplain in the State School does the same things that a parish priest does. He leads his people in the worship of God, he teaches and preaches, he administers the Sacraments, he counsels and consoles, he advises and exhorts—and he gets involved in unimaginable problems. The reason for this similarity is obvious: both men are engaged in the business of saving souls. The setting in which this business is carried on differs considerably in the two cases, however.

I was not surprised at the difference in the setting—just awed and bewildered by it. What really surprised me, though, was the doubt expressed by some that I was still engaged in the same business. I guess there will always be people who wonder what any clergyman does all day long —like the ones who express genuine disbelief when they discover that the pastor has not just been sitting there waiting for them to ring the front doorbell.

Even though my previous acquaintance with retarded

children had been negligible, I had never questioned the fact that their souls needed saving. Now, not only the Church but even the State has acknowledged that fact by the provision of full-time Chaplains for these institutions.

While the severely retarded may not require any spiritual care beyond the administering of Baptism, the remainder of them need the same ministrations as the rest of us. Depending on their degree of retardation, it is true that the spiritual needs of some are very simple. But many of them are able to participate quite fully in the practice of their religion. I found that out the very first weekend I spent with them.

It is perhaps understandable, then, that I became chagrined when, in those early days, I would meet an old friend who could not understand "what you do all day." One went so far as to suggest that the maintenance of a Chaplaincy is completely futile by saying, "Those kids don't need a Chaplain; they're all saved already." I am sure he was laboring under the delusion that these institutions are filled with custodial cases, all profoundly retarded, who require nothing more than to be baptized, fed, bedded, and medicated.

There are countless patients in our State Schools who are not at all educable, not even trainable. They are the people who used to be called custodial cases back in the days when these places were called asylums. Now it is recognized that these retardates are considerably more than vegetables and can respond to programs of intensive care and benefit from projects like "Activities of Daily Living." But you do not have to spend much time in one of these places to discover that hundreds of others have a lot of other requirements, too.

I was discovering it. As soon as I was able to go beyond my own front porch without getting lost, I began to explore the interior of the buildings. One of the duties of the Chaplains of the State Schools is the regular visitation of all the wards. The ward is the home of the patient, the place where he eats and sleeps and hangs his hat. The homemakers are the ward attendants, the people who live with the patients and take the immediate place of their parents. Each ward is in charge of a staff attendant or a head nurse, and a group of several wards is under the direction of a supervisor. This entire division of employees is known as Nursing Service or Ward Service and is directed by the Chief Supervising Nurse.

I was already getting to know many of the people in the hierarchy of Nursing Service as a result of my ward rounds and also because these people have the closest relationship with the patients. The attendant is the one who regularly fulfills the everyday wants and needs of the patient. And it is an inspiration to see with what diligence and devotion this relationship is carried out.

The ward is the basic and the most important unit in an institution of this kind. Therefore, thirty-one wards here occupy the most space and absorb by far the largest part of the personnel. Supervisors' offices, nurses' clinics, and doctors' offices are located here and there along the corridors. You might say that all these boys and girls have their own family doctor. Each area has its ward physician and clinical nurse, and Medical Service works hand in hand with Nursing Service in the day-to-day care of the patient.

Furthermore, the appetites of these children are anything but retarded, and the employees have to eat, too. So it is not surprising that Food Service should be a huge, active, and complex department in a place like this.

All these facilities you would expect to find in the State School, even if you considered it merely a custodial asylum for the profoundly retarded, who need only to be fed, bedded, medicated—and baptized. But as I pushed further and further into the interior, more and more of the requirements of the retarded were revealed.

In those first few weeks I was constantly uncovering some new aspect of the patients' lives. As I traveled from ward to ward, I found classrooms, craftrooms, playrooms, and workshops scattered throughout all the buildings. I saw patients reading and writing, sawing and sewing, studying and working, and playing. And their myriad activities told me that they needed not only shelter, food, clothing, medication—and sanctification—but also education, recreation, and occupation. They were getting all these things at the hands of experts in each field, a large corps of specially trained men and women who make up the Education, Recreation, and Occupational Therapy Departments. No wonder this is called a school!

Nobody was learning more than the new Chaplain. Among other things, I had collected a few more names. Dr. Edward Stevenson, a smiling, soft-spoken man with a real sense of humor, is the Assistant Clinical Director, whose job includes supervision of the vital department known as the Medical Staff. The Chief Supervising Nurse, who directs the ubiquitous Nursing Service, is a charming and competent lady by the name of Ora Cutting. No less charming, and with as many years of experience, is the Director of Education, Geraldine Collins. Her cohorts in the training and education field are the Occupational Therapy Supervisor, Chester Pelis, a big, brawny fellow with just as big a heart, and Marguerite Mechie, a cordial little woman who supervises the Recreation Department. These are the people who spark the manifold activities I was witnessing in wards, clinics, classrooms, play areas, and workshops.

But patient activity is not limited to these areas. Wherever I went, I met boys and girls coming and going—to and from the boilerhouse, the sewing room, the storehouse, and the laundry, to the shops of the plumber, the engineer, the tinsmith, and the electrician, and to the kitchens, dining rooms, offices, and apartments. Industry was contributing its share to the training and education of another large segment of the population—and receiving a handsome share of work in return.

Here was another army of men and women helping these boys and girls to lead full and purposeful lives. I learned that they were being directed by such people as Aleta Och, Supervising Housekeeper, who manages to be all over the institution at once with her shrewd and sympathetic advice on a million household problems; or Don Scott, Head Stationary Engineer, who quietly and calmly keeps everything running and functioning; or Ella Lawrence, Food Service Manager, who feeds almost 5,000 people with a smile.

When the awareness of this tremendous network of activity began to dawn on me, I realized that two elements especially were involved in huge quantities: manpower and supplies. Those are the chief requirements for waging a war. And that is what it is, a war against mental retardation. And it is being fought on every front, with companies of brave men and women under well-seasoned officers, using every conceivable kind of ammunition and strategy and tactic. The general who marshals the manpower is Dr. Murray Bergman, Assistant Administrative Director. Francis Rockwood, Business Officer, is in charge of equipment and supplies.

Why, this place is not so strange, after all! It is a battlefield—the very setting every clergyman is used to. He is pledged to save souls, to fight the good fight, to wage war against sin, to do battle against the powers of darkness. In the State School he is the Chaplain on the spiritual front. His immediate superior officer is the Director, who is chief of staff for the entire operation and guides the plans for all the maneuvers. How appropriate that his office should be located at the Front!

VIII

JOSÉ FELIZ

LITTLE did I think, as the vision of this mighty battle against the powers of mental darkness passed before my eyes, that soon I not only would be engaged in a war of wits but would also be on the verge of physical combat.

As much as the institution resembles a battlefield, I was consoled to note some encouraging dissimilarities. The fight cannot be classed as a cold war, because we actually come to grips with the enemy. But neither is there any danger that the field will be strewed with dead bodies. No matter what the weaknesses in our forces may be, none of us joining the battle could ever be overpowered by the opposition, which has already claimed its victims. On the other hand, we can never hope to be absolute victors, since there is no possibility of completely vanquishing mental retardation. Nevertheless, it was cheering to know that so many on our side had finally infiltrated the enemy's ranks and that little victories were constantly being won.

Thoughts of this kind led me to a strange paradox. For

the priest, the lines are clearly drawn: he is fighting on the side of God against Satan, the deadly foe. But in this new arena of combat, he is lined up, still with God, but also against an evil permitted by God. The Creator sends children into the world, victims of mental retardation, and here we are fighting it. A slight problem, really, I decided. *All* evil, against which we do battle, is *permitted* by God, but it is a *result* of sin, the sin of Adam. And sin is the weapon of the Devil. So whether we are warring against sin or plague or famine—or mental retardation—the battle is truly against evil. That means God is on our side—as long as we are on His. Well, you can—

The doorbell! It brought me back to reality with a jolt, because in two weeks, it was the first time it had sounded after supper. Standing at the door was a handsome husky redhead who introduced himself as an attendant from East Dorm 3. Behind him was another big fellow, rawboned and blond, with heavy glasses and a sagging jaw.

"My name is Bill Peck," said the attendant, "and this is one of our new boys on East 3, Don Carr. Don has a problem, and we thought maybe you could help him."

"I'll be glad to try. Come in."

Bill and Don sat across the desk from me, and Don did the talking. He said he was very upset; I found it hard to believe, because of the slow, unfeeling drawl in which he spoke. There was not the slightest trace of emotion on his face when he told me why he was upset: "Because they sent me here for burning down a barn."

"Did you burn down a barn?"

"No. That's why I'm upset."

It was obvious to me that the fellow was retarded—

64

probably only mildly. And that surely must be the reason why he was sent here.

"Who sent you here for burning down the barn?"

"The judge."

The judge? Is that what he said: "The judge"?

"Yes, the judge in court."

Oh, no! This is not a criminal institution. People aren't sentenced to this place. He must be mistaken. The attendant will know. I shall speak to him privately. Don can wait in the chapel. It cannot be true.

"Yes, it is, Father. This boy was committed here by the court for arson. I don't think he's really guilty, but that's why he's here."

Good grief! You mean we accept criminals here? I know I have to fight evil, but do I have to fight crime?

"Oh, sure, Father, patients are committed here by the courts for all kinds of offenses."

An atom bomb couldn't have shaken my battleground with a more shattering force. "Are you sure?"

"Yes, some of our boys are here for stealing and fighting and—"

Oh, my gosh! Are we safe? There are votive lights burning in the chapel. Maybe Don will burn the place down. Maybe—maybe I'm not among friends, after all.

"You seem surprised, Father."

Surprised? I am shaken to the roots. Here, I just had myself convinced that I was waging war on a nice peaceful battlefield when a new enemy rears its ugly head. Criminals! And the doors of the wards are not even locked. No bars on the windows. Lord, help us!

The attendant does not seem to be a bit perturbed—as

though arsonists and thieves and gangsters are a commonplace with him. But it cannot be that way. I have not
been here very long, but I have not heard of a single out-
break of violence, nor have I seen any violence. In fact,
things have been much more placid and serene than I
could have hoped for. It is ridiculous. Facts would seem
to contradict these wild notions.

Well, there is no use arguing the case now. I shall just
do my best to calm the patient for the time being, until I
get a chance to do some investigating.

It was not difficult. Don was already the calmest upset
person I had ever seen. I decided that he was pretty cold-
blooded for an arsonist. Indeed, he impressed me as so meek
and languid that I wondered if he could be persuaded to
light a match, let alone a barn.

After a few words about accepting God's will and trust-
ing in Him, I promised the boy (twenty-six years old, his
card said) that I would check into the matter and see
what I could do.

When Bill and Don left, I made out my daily record.
(The state requires a monthly report of the activities of
each department.) I was tempted to enter the item "Interviewed first criminal." But no—it cannot be true. I do not
believe that fellow started a fire. And even if he did, it
would not be a crime, because he is retarded. He *could not*
have been sentenced here for arson. As a matter of fact,
he was not. I lost no time the next morning in tracking
down the facts. Dr. Stevenson, who is in charge of admission procedures, lost no time in putting me on the right
track.

Don Carr *had* been sent here by a judge, he told me, and

he *was* accused of arson; but it is not a sentence, and he is not a criminal, and this is not a penal institution.

Well, thank God for all that! But what about all the other "thieves" and "robbers" and "gangsters" in our midst?

Dr. Stevenson laughed. He could see that I was upset—and not quietly upset as my arsonist friend had been. He would have a much bigger job calming me down than I had had with Don.

"It's true," he said, "that some of our patients have got into trouble out in the community. But you must remember that the retarded are very easily led, and very often the trouble is really instigated by someone else—of normal intelligence."

Another sigh of relief.

"If a retardate gets involved in some social problem, he may be taken to court. When it is established that he is retarded, the judge may *commit* him to one of the State Schools. He isn't sentenced, and the offense is only the occasion of the commitment."

More relief.

"No one is sent here for punishment, but for training and rehabilitation—and very often for his own protection, more than for the protection of society."

Still more. Good old Dr. Stevenson! What a safety valve he proved to be that morning. So people like Don are committed by the court because of their retardation.

"That's right. It's called a court certification. We simply admit such patients on the recommendation of the judge, instead of at the request of their parents or the certification of a physician or psychologist."

Well that is easy enough to understand and is certainly a lot less disturbing concept than the one I had last night. So none of these patients is really dangerous then?

"You haven't a thing to worry about, Father."

I did not. I did not worry after that enlightening interview with Dr. Stevenson.

I would have, if I could have foreseen the events of the next Sunday. Fortunately, I had to wait until Sunday to see what would happen. So I did not worry.

Instead, I continued to acquaint myself with my environment. As I got to know more and more of the patients, I became more firmly convinced that they all were quite harmless. The fears of Thursday night were soon completely dispelled.

Oh, there were distressing sights which it would take some time for me to get used to: the hydrocephalics and spastics and the otherwise physically handicapped. There were problems which I would have to learn to cope with, too. Not all the brighter patients are always content and satisfied. Some of them complain about not having visitors, about not being treated fairly, about not being "paroled." Others are picked on by their fellow patients, or do not like their jobs, or cannot get along with a certain employee. But such things, I soon discovered, are just an indication of their approach to normalcy. The more retarded they are, the fewer problems they have. It is the normal person who has the problems.

Most of these patients are happy-go-lucky, demanding nothing more than a little affection, a little attention, a little token of esteem. And how easy it is to offer these

things to people who are as friendly and likable as most
retardates are!

It soon became apparent that my chief difficulty would
be not the lack of affection and attention, but of tokens.
These boys and girls long to be given things. They yearn
for little possessions. A tiny picture will light up their faces
with joy. The simplest item will cause them to exclaim,
"Oh, ain't that beautiful!" If the picture happens to be a
holy one or the item happens to be a religious one, it
immediately becomes a precious treasure.

My every appearance in a group of patients was becoming a signal for a deluge of requests for medals,
rosaries, statues, or just "a holy." I was able to satisfy most
of these demands, since I had found a supply of little
religious articles in one of the file drawers at my office. It
bothered me, however, because I had to say no so often to
the question, "Have you got a Bible?" After I discovered
that "Bible" simply meant any kind of prayer book and
that even the most illiterate prized such a possession, my
friend-making ability was considerably enhanced.

Making friends with the retarded is ordinarily an easy
matter. My encounter with José Feliz was about to demon-
strate this fact. But José Feliz was also about to provoke
anew some of the misgivings that had been aroused by the
Don Carr incident. I had talked with Don again, and our
relationship had become quite cordial. I had also met José
and was impressed by his quiet, friendly manner.

José was a tall, slim boy of about nineteen, with a dark
complexion and an intense look in his eyes. Our one meeting was casual, but as I recalled later, he seemed to be very
preoccupied. He was only mildly retarded, and he had

made a capable assistant to Mr. Babcock, who managed the Boys' Club. My talk with the boy was brief and routine and quickly forgotten, since there seemed to be nothing very unusual about him.

But there was. I learned that, through the harrowing experience of the Sunday afternoon which would have worried me decidedly, could I have foreseen it.

It was the first Sunday of August. The whole month since my arrival had been just as hot and humid as the day I had first set foot on these precincts. This Sunday was no exception. It was sweltering. Some friends had dropped in after lunch to pay a visit. They were the first guests in my new home, and I invited them to stay for supper. I had so much to tell them.

They never heard it. Greetings had hardly been exchanged when the phone rang. It was the Charge on East Dorm 1. He sounded excited.

"Can you come down right away?"

Of course, I could.

"One of our boys has gone on a rampage and locked himself in a room. He says he won't talk to anyone but you."

It was José. He felt he could trust me. Would I please come?

"I'll be right there."

Grabbing my monstrous ring of keys, I excused myself from my company and told them I would return in a few minutes.

The East Dorm is located on the big circle, opposite the West, just a stone's throw from my place, so I walked. The sun was beating down unmercifully, and in my rush, I was dripping perspiration by the time I reached the building's front door. I hurried more out of a desire to get back to my guests than because I thought it was demanded by the situation.

This building houses four wards of male patients. Similar in arrangement to the West Dorm, Wards 1 and 3 are located on the first and second floors to the right of the main entrance, while Wards 2 and 4 are down and up to the left. I had also learned that Wards 1 and 3 in both buildings are for brighter patients, working boys and school boys, and that the boys on 2 and 4 are more re-tarded. In general, the age of the patients in the West Dorm is lower than that in the East. All the schoolboys are, therefore, in the West Dorm. Boys like José Feliz and Don Carr, who work in the various industries and services, are on East 1 and 3.

Casting quick greetings right and left to the patients I passed on the way, I hustled into the lobby, past the visitors' room, and was soon at the door of East Dorm 1.

As I opened the door, I froze in my tracks. The corridor was lined with people. The first ones who caught my eye were two state troopers.

State troopers? What for? They were not just lounging or passing the time of day. They were rigid and ready for action.

I quickly noted, also, two of our own patrolmen—in the same posture.

An armed guard! What was going on?

Several attendants were strung along the hallway, too, and a few other people I could not—or did not take time to—identify. Among this tense cohort, one other person stood out: Dr. Henne, the Director.

And what is *he* doing here on Sunday? Saturday and Sunday are always pass days for office and administrative personnel. Only an emergency would bring him here today.

That is what it was. All the questions swarmed into my head at once. And they all were answered just as quickly by Joe Stewart, who was in charge that day. From among the motionless figures, he stepped up to me and explained in an excited gush of words.

"José's barricaded in there ... armed with a shovel ... took a swipe at me ... threatening to kill himself ... two hours ... won't listen to anybody ... wants you."

I had joined the crowd. Rigid and tense, I was speechless.

But I had to talk. To José. Through the door. Quietly, kindly, persuasively.

Relax. Compose yourself. Mop your brow. Pray! Yes: "Dear Lord, help me." Speak.

"José? José, this is Father Bauer. I've come to help you. Can you hear me, José?"

No answer.

"José, will you let me in?"

"Don't go in there, Father!" It was a trooper. "He's armed."

"But we have to get him out, don't we?"

"Well—be careful!"

So none of these patients is really dangerous? Oh-h-h! I'll try again.

"José, I'm your friend. I want to help you. Please speak to me."

"I won't go to the South Dorm!" It was a frenzied scream from beyond the door. I couldn't recognize it as the voice of José Feliz, and I couldn't understand what it meant.

Noticing my puzzled expression, Dr. Henne, who had moved next to me, explained: "He was seen breaking into the Boys' Club, took refuge here when the patrolman gave chase, has a terrible fear of detention at South Dorm."

A resident ward for profoundly retarded older male patients, South Dorm is one of our two locked wards. I knew that emotionally disturbed and problem boys, such as constant elopers, were sent there as a protection for themselves and others. Nobody likes to be locked up. I did not blame José for his fear. I must be very gentle.

"José, if you let me in, we can talk it over. I only want to help you. You know I'm your friend."

There was not a sound from any of the people standing in the corridor—or from José.

"You can't stay in there forever, José. Won't you please open the door?"

"They'll take me to the South Dorm!"

"José, I won't take you to the South Dorm. Just let me in, so I can talk to you. I promise you I won't let anyone else come in." Lord, help us, please.

That did it.

"All right—but just you."

"Yes, José, just me."

From inside the room there was much ramming and banging and scuffling. What in the world is in there?

73

Mr. Stewart answered my question: "It's the soiled laundry room. There's a heap of dirty laundry and a couple of hampersful in there."

Indeed, there was. After what seemed an interminable length of time, the door began to move in little fits and starts. Something was still jamming it. Finally, it was jerked open about six inches and stopped. I pushed, but with no result.

"Will you open it a little more, José?"

"I can't."

He can't? Then *I* can't get in. This hulk will never fit through that little slot. Someone came to my aid, and the two of us managed to shove the door another inch or two. I decided to try.

Somehow I managed to wiggle through the constricted opening and to climb over the huge hamper into a pile of steaming towels, sheets, and clothes. Already bathed in sweat, I found the airless four by four room unbearable.

Behind a mountain of soiled laundry stood José clenching the handle of a huge shovel, with the look of a hunted beast in his eyes. He said nothing and moved not a muscle.

When I managed to get fully inside the room, I noticed an iron ladder attached to the wall and leading to a hatch in the ceiling. It was the only opening in the tiny room, except for the door. Near the top of the ladder the boy had fastened his belt to one of the rungs. Beside it, securely tied by one corner, hung a sheet. The suicide instruments! And in his hands, the murder weapon.

José was not in a talkative mood. Nor was I, really. All he would say was, "I am not going to the South Dorm."

After much reasoning and pleading and cajoling, the

74

magic words finally came again: "I promise you that you will not have to go to the South Dorm."

The trump was played. José handed me the shovel and climbed out of his foxhole after me. What the next move would be, I could not imagine. I did not have to. As soon as the boy stepped into the corridor, one of the troopers latched onto him and headed him for the attendants' office. In the routine line of duty he was about to gather data from the "culprit." A sinking feeling hit my stomach. This boy is as taut as a rubber band at the breaking point. He cannot endure a questionnaire. God, help me to say the right thing!

"Officer, could you please postpone that for a few minutes? I think José would like to talk to me a little more. Would you mind if we just sat down together someplace for a little while?"

"*Alone*, Father?" The trooper sensed his duty.

But I sensed mine, too. He was sworn to protect the interests of all concerned, including mine. At the moment my only concern was José. I knew he was far from reconciled. I knew he trusted me. But I was not sure he was ready to trust anyone else.

The trooper looked at Dr. Henne, who had followed us into the office. "Is it all right, Doctor?"

I had already learned that our Director is a cautious man. He does not make a move without considering all the angles. His glance shifted from the officer to me to José. He hesitated. José had resumed his stolid stance, and the hunted look had returned to his eyes. I could see that I had made my point with Dr. Henne. He conceded, but with a precaution.

75

"Yes," he said, "I think Father should talk with José a bit more. But I'll go along."

The office on a ward is always humming with activity, so Mr. Stewart ushered the three of us into the sewing and storage room across the hall. On the way the Director asked me how I had persuaded the patient to leave the laundry room.

"I promised him he wouldn't have to go to the South Dorm."

He was stunned.

"But you can't do that. He must go to the South Dorm. This boy is terribly disturbed. He is a danger to himself and to others. It is my duty to confine him."

The sinking feeling hit me again. José trusted me, and I had made a promise to him. Divine assistance, please!

The attendant left, and the three of us were seated in the sewing room. Dr. Henne and I tried every possible approach, but José would not budge. He sat stiffly and defiantly without uttering a word or batting an eyelash. In desperation, I finally grasped at another straw.

"Doctor, may I speak with you alone for a moment?"

That posed another problem. We both could not leave the room. Fortunately, there was another door which led to a little antechamber. The attendant had locked the entrance door on his way out, so the Director stepped into the adjoining room with me.

"I think I can get José to talk if he is absolutely alone with me," I ventured.

"But I *can't* leave you alone with him."

"Then we have arrived at a stalemate."

Dr. Henne is not only cautious, but shrewd as well.

"All right," he said. "I will leave the room, but you must leave the door open."

"Unlocked—but closed," I interjected.

"Well— Yes. But promise me that you will call for help immediately if you need it."

"I will."

"And you must tell him that he has to go to the South Dorm."

Dear God! Yes, that is what I must do.

"All right," I said without an ounce of conviction.

As the Director reluctantly joined the group out in the corridor, I turned to my impossible task. José had not moved a muscle. He was seated next to a worktable, staring at the door. I pulled my chair up to the other side of the table and invited him to swing around to face me. To my astonishment, he readily complied, but without shifting his eyes from the door.

Between us on the table was a heavy wooden pool-ball box. Instinctively José's right hand clutched it and drew it toward him.

His new weapon! Oh, Lord, I need Your help!

I thought it would never come. Try as I might, I could not get a word out of José. And I could not get the box out of his fist—or his eyes off the door.

That's it! The divine assistance had arrived. The door. His weapon is a defense against the armed guard outside. But I had promised to leave the door unlocked. I had also promised the boy—

"José, if I lock the door, will you give me the box and speak to me?"

77

For the first time since we had left the laundry room, the boy spoke. "Yes."

Thank God!

Certain of the consternation it would cause in the corridor, I resolutely inserted my master key in the door, turned it, and left the rest of the keys dangling from their ring. By the time I returned to the table, José's gaze had drifted from the door. His head and shoulders sagged; he handed me the box—and began to cry.

The Lord be praised! I knew the day was won. I felt that this boy was the type to whom spiritual motivation would appeal, if only I could get through. Until now nothing could. The psychological barrier had been impregnable. I was hoping that his tears would wash it away.

They did. In a few moments the "culprit" had *agreed* to go to the South Dorm. He also agreed to talk with the state trooper. My own agreement was a safe one this time, I knew: I would personally accompany José to the South Dorm and visit him every day while he was there.

Before I left him in his new quarters, José asked me to hear his Confession and to bring him Communion the next morning. No one could have thought of a happier ending to the events of the afternoon.

As I turned the key in the front door of the South Dorm and turned my steps back toward my own door, the thought of home jarred me.

I have guests waiting for me! I told them I would be back in a few minutes, and that was two and a half hours ago!

Externally, I was drenched with perspiration and completely wilted from the heat. Internally, I felt a glow of satisfaction over the accomplishment of the afternoon. It was all but drowned, however, by the haunting recurrence of the words which Dr. Stevenson had uttered so confidently only a few days before: "You haven't a thing to worry about, Father."

At that point, I could not agree with that statement. Nevertheless, this was not the time to worry or disagree. As I approached the Moss Building, I saw that my guests' car was still in the parking area. They had been gracious enough to wait for me all this time. Now I must be a gracious host.

Summoning up every ounce of energy, determination, and courage that remained to me, I opened the door, turned and took one more look at my battlefield, pushed the fear and worry and disagreement back onto the front porch, and closed the door on them. Then I stopped in the chapel.

"Thank you, Lord, for all the help you gave me this afternoon. Just one more favor, please? Kindly take care of the things I left on the front porch till tomorrow for me. I have to take care of my guests now. Thank you, Lord."

IX

LESSON FROM THE PSYCHIATRIST

THE next morning I looked out of my window at the two empty reservoirs across the street—that is what my "swimming pools" turned out to be, relics of the days when the institution had to provide its own water supply. They made me think of all the water that had gone over the dam during the last month. How swiftly the stream of events had flowed, and how its currents had shifted my course to and fro!

I remembered that first day, when I had been lost and had caught sight of the patrolman. I had wondered then if the policeman had much violence to contend with. But I had immediately dismissed the thought. I had decided that all the patients were quite harmless and friendly and well behaved. Then just when I had been thoroughly convinced of that, Don Carr had turned up and brought visions of terror into my soul. These visions, however, had been promptly dispelled by the explanation and reassurance of Dr. Stevenson. But the tranquillity had been of short duration. Yesterday had turned out to be a first-class nightmare.

Well, I cannot become involved in an analysis of José Feliz now. I left my problems on the front porch, and they will have to stay there until after Mass. That is when I shall be taking Holy Communion to José. And that will be time enough to consider him.

When I got to the South Dorm, I found him waiting for me in the visitors' room. He was kneeling at a chair, praying devoutly. He seemed very calm and peaceful, but the intense look I noted in his eyes when I first met him was still there. The wild glare of yesterday was gone, however, and he looked like the José I at first thought he was.

That is the way I found him again after breakfast, when I returned to talk with him. He was not happy about being in the South Dorm, but there was no sign of rebellion. In fact, he was full of remorse.

I was full of questions. Why had he gone into such a frenzy yesterday?

"I was scared."

Of what?

"Of the cop, of the South Dorm, of everybody."

And why, above all else, had he broken into the Boys' Club?

"To feed the cat."

To feed the *cat?*

"Yes, Father. Mr. Babcock has a cat, and I like it very much. I knew he wouldn't be here on Sunday, and I didn't want the cat to be hungry."

But you must have known it was wrong to break in?

"I didn't break in. I unlocked the window before Mr. Babcock closed up Saturday night."

So you went through the window?

"And Mr. Dean saw me crawling out."

But why didn't you tell him what happened? Why did you run away?

"I was scared."

And the shovel?

"I didn't want to go to the South Dorm."

But is that the right way to act?

"No, Father."

And you were going to hang yourself?

"Yes, Father."

Why?

"I thought it would be better than being locked up."

Is that what God thinks?

"No, Father. It's bad. It's all bad, and I'm sorry. I just lost my head. I won't ever do it again."

I was sure he would not. He was so sincere, so contrite, so meek. My heart ached for him. But I had to tell him that I hoped his stay in the South Dorm would be a lesson to him. I had to exhort him firmly to behave himself, so that he could get out soon and prove himself. And I counseled him to say his prayers and to beg God's help for the present and the future.

As I was leaving, the Charge told me that José had given them no trouble since he had come to the South Dorm. He was very docile and cooperative. Good! Then he will be out in a few days.

"No, he won't, Father." That was the ward physician speaking. I met him as I turned to leave, voicing my hope. His name is Semchyshyn, the doctor in charge of the East and South Dorms. He is a husky, imposing Ukrainian, who takes an intense interest in his work and whose voice commands immediate attention. Like all the physicians here, he is also a psychiatrist. A jovial man by nature, he can scare the daylights out of you with his expressive explanation of a problem.

He scared the daylights out of me that morning without trying, since I was still jumpy from the ordeal of the previous day. "We'll have to keep him here awhile, till we can decide what to do," he added.

Well, that won't take very long. He's all settled down already.

"Oh, no, he isn't. This is only a temporary phase. And we have to hold a psychiatric conference on the case."

Good grief! I know the fellow had us all terrorized yesterday. But he's as meek as a lamb this morning. Why make such an issue of it? Can't we just forgive him? He's learned his lesson. I'm sure he won't ever cut loose like that again.

"But he will, Father."

He promised me he wouldn't.

"But you don't understand. This boy is psychotic."

Psychotic? I thought he was retarded.

"He is, but he is psychotic, too."

You mean he's mentally ill?

"That's right. It doesn't happen very often, but it has happened to him, and he needs special treatment."

Psychiatric treatment?

"Yes. But not the kind of psychiatric treatment we employ here. The purpose of the State Schools is to provide therapy for the mentally retarded, but not for the mentally ill. This is one of those rare cases which is out of our line. You understand, Father?"

Yes, thank God, I understand one more thing. Poor José! I understand that he has a double handicap. So many of these people do, but with the rest of them, only one affliction is mental; the other is physical. In José's case, both handicaps are of the mind. Dr. Henne knew that yesterday. That is why he was so determined.

And I understand another thing. I understand why Dr. Stevenson assured me that I have nothing to worry about. Violence is not a part of mental retardation. Nor is crime. Still, violent or criminal acts may occur among the retarded, just as in any other segment of humanity. They are simply some of the evil which God permits. And it is consoling to realize that the retarded are less to blame for them than the rest of us.

"You'll get tons of it, right there on the job," the Bishop had retorted when I protested my lack of clinical training. I was getting it, perhaps not by the ton, but it seemed that almost every incident was providing me with quite a heap.

I thanked Dr. Semchyshyn for his enlightenment and then stopped in the dayroom to see the regular residents of the South Dorm. A little fellow by the name of Jake, all smiles, came up to shake my hand and pat me on the back. A couple of other patients said, "Hello," and one even said, "Good-morning, Father." Aside from that, there was little recognition made of my presence. Even though I felt they had no need of my blessing, I begged the benediction of the Father, the Son, and the Holy Ghost upon these profoundly retarded men as I let myself out with the king-size master key.

I thought of the moment the day before when I had done the same thing. That bunch of keys seemed to weigh a ton then, like the terrible burdens that were weighing on my mind. But now, even though I felt sad, the keys seemed much lighter. Yesterday their clang sounded like the gong of doom. Today they are the tinkle of a bell, because the burdens have been lightened. I guess a little talk with the psychiatrist is good for anybody.

X

COMING AND GOING

DISTURBING elements are usually magnified by un-familiar circumstances. We can sleep soundly through the clatter of traffic on the street where we live and yet be kept awake all night by the chirping of a cricket on the hearth of our uncle's farm. The unexpected can have the same effect.

The 519 acres of my new domain were strange territory to me for many weeks. And the occupants of these acres are a very special segment of humanity. Many of the pro-grams, procedures, and practices prevailing among them are baffling to the newcomer. It was little wonder, then, that the Carr and Feliz incidents shocked me unduly and gave rise to unfounded misgivings.

When you view the matter disinterestedly and unemo-tionally, what is unusual about a boy's being psychotic? Or why should a court commitment to an institution be viewed with alarm? The courts are constantly declaring offenders insane; why not retarded? And all kinds of people suffer mental derangements; why not the retarded? Like the cricket on the hearth, these discoveries merely demand a little reorientation.

Gradually I was becoming oriented. Day by day, more and more of the mysteries in my office began to unfold. Day by day, my acquaintance with patients and employees was broadening. Day by day, the operation of the institution was becoming more understandable.

Red tape is a common commodity in modern civilization. But nowhere is it more common than in a complex organism like the State School. And again, I found, you can get pitifully tangled up when it is a brand new skein of tape.

Records, reports, and requisitions surrounded me on every side. I decided to unravel first the ones that concerned me most: the patients' file cards, transfer cards, ward checklists, and church record books. These records encompass such items as psychometric evaluations and spiritual prognoses, which are so important in determining who is capable of going to church, of receiving the Sacraments, or of benefiting from religious instruction.

The file card is the most helpful of all the Chaplain's records, I discovered. It gives all the essential facts about the patient: name, age, parentage, origin, MA, IQ, Sacraments received, physical handicaps, and the Chaplain's evaluation.

I knew where the final item originated, because I interviewed each new admission shortly after his arrival, in order to get acquainted with him and to make that evaluation. The chief objectives of my own admission procedure are to determine whether the patient is baptized and has made his First Communion and to decide whether he is able to go to church and to catechism class. But that information is just a drop in the bucket. Where does all the rest come from?

As my orientation process continued, the general admission procedure became clear. It involves a generous length of red tape, which, however, unravels to a great extent the history and the mystery of each new admission.

After the preliminary arrangements are made, usually by the parents or a social agency, the child is brought to the school. The preliminary arrangements may have included the certification of a physician, a psychologist, or a judge and an interview with one of our Social Workers. These may, in turn, have been preceded by physical, psychiatric, and psychological examinations and tests and by a clinical diagnosis.

The Social Service interview takes place upon the child's arrival, if it was not conducted previously. As our liaison with the community, Social Service obtains from the parents or a community agency all the available pertinent facts which will help us in evaluating, classifying, and treating the new admission. This history and the certification papers are the beginning of the patient's personal file.

Following the work of the Social Service Department, the Medical Service goes into action. The child receives a complete physical and psychiatric examination from the Admitting Physician, who adds to the file his first medical record.

The next phase in the admission procedure is the adjustment of the patient to institutional routine on the admission ward. There the nurses and attendants strive to take over where the parents left off, providing for the everyday needs of the child. X rays, photographs, and laboratory tests occupy some of his first few days in his new home and add to his growing file.

Then comes the psychometric evaluation. The Associate or Senior Clinical Psychologist administers a series of psychological tests, by which he is able to determine the intelligence quotient (IQ), mental age (MA), and various intellectual abilities. The patient's file grows thicker.

After a few weeks the Admitting Physician, acting upon all the information that has been gathered, assigns the well-documented individual to the residential ward best suited to his age, mental level, and physical condition.

Along with him go his personal belongings, his medication record, clothing list, initial fact sheet, continued notes, and religious transfer card. The transfer card was made out by the Chaplain at the time of his spiritual evaluation of the patient and will tell the Charge on the new ward whether the boy or girl should go to church or class or receive the Sacraments. His continued notes are a day-by-day account of his progress, started by the Charge on the admission ward and to be continued by the new Charge. The initial fact sheet, compiled by the Social Worker and the Admitting Physician, contains the basic facts that will be helpful to all who deal with the patient.

Now the child is settled in his new home. The attendants on the residential ward continue the parental care inaugurated on the admission ward, and the family doctor takes over in the person of the Ward Physician.

But the admission procedure is not yet completed. Very

soon the Training Coordination Committee will meet to consider the role this new member is to assume in our family. Composed of the head or representative of each department, the committee, under the guidance of the Director of Education and on the recommendation of the Clinical Psychologist, decides whether the child should be enrolled in an educational, occupational therapy, or recreation program or in a combination of such programs. Or they may determine that the boy or girl may profit more from ward activity, industrial training, activities of daily living, or simply nursing care.

In the meantime, the new arrival, further documented with a baptismal certificate secured by the Chaplain, has already been integrated into the religious program. He may be going to church and to religious instructions at the hall and the chapel. Or he may have religious services and classes right on his own ward if he is nonambulatory.

Within the period of a month the average patient has been assimilated into the life of the institution, and his physical, intellectual, spiritual, medical, social, and emotional needs are being fulfilled by the countless members of his huge new family.

But he may not continue indefinitely as a member of that family. The training, education, treatment, and habilitation he receives here may make it possible for him to return to the community and assume some responsibility as a vital member of society. He was probably introduced to the institution by the Social Service Department. When one of his periodic reevaluations indicates that he is ready, Social Service will take over again and return him to the community by placing him in one of our colonies or in a sheltered workshop or boarding home or by securing a job for him. Such placement is what I heard the patients calling parole.

If it is judged that the patient has made sufficient progress either within the institution or in a community placement situation, he may be discharged either to his own custody or returned to his own family.

In my file drawer, I noticed almost as many cards for discharged patients as for current ones. Many of them had gone full circle. I wondered about my houseboy. He seemed so capable. Couldn't he be discharged? As time went on, I wondered about others. Why couldn't they make their way, out in society?

I did not have to ask, because I soon realized that boys and girls were not only going out, but coming back in. I made a practice of having a counseling session with every patient before he left for community placement. When I realized that some of them were not staying out, I began to interview them again upon their return. In some cases they come back because they get into trouble of some kind or another. But many times the reason is simply that they cannot cope with the situation. They may not be able to control themselves, or their money, or their relationships with others. Some who fare quite well in the institutional setting, with all its special aids and facilities, may fail when they are released from its protective environment. My interviews often revealed these facts.

Not being a psychiatrist, however, I discovered that my interviews did not always disclose all the facts. That was what happened with José Feliz. Even after I was advised of his mental illness, I was unable to detect it in my conversations with him. But the psychiatric interview made it clear to the doctors. And their psychiatric conference resulted in a decision: José, too, was to be discharged—but to a state hospital.

I was seeing them come and go. For some, the coming is hard and the going is easy. For others, the reverse is true. One of our tasks, I began to see, is to make both the coming and the going as easy as possible—and the staying easier still.

XI

BEHIND THE HEADLINES

MY admission interviews took me to three particular buildings: the Children's Building, where all patients under five are admitted; the Boys' Hospital, and the Girls' Hospital, where the male and female admission wards are located. The last two buildings also house the facilities for treating those who are acutely ill. So my visits to the sick added to the number of calls at those places.

While the required contact with the newly admitted and the sick patients put these wards at the head of my list, nevertheless, I was getting to know every type of patient from my regular ward rounds. By interviewing the newly admitted and those being paroled, I learned the joys and the sorrows of their comings and goings.

I remember one very spastic girl by the name of Eloise, who would say nothing but "I want to go home," in response to every question I asked at the time of her admission. And Laurie, who left nothing but troubles behind her, kept saying, "I'm going to run away." The only response of another new admission, a nine-year-old boy named Patsy, was an interminable earsplitting scream.

On the other hand, Cynthia, a cheerful teen-ager, told me that she was glad she had finally come to a place where she could learn something, because she had had such difficulties in school. And Donny was all set to get to work learning a trade, so he could go out and earn a living. In my first visits with the severely retarded, too, I was being greeted by smiles just as often as by tears.

Those being placed in a community status of one kind or another are invariably happy at the prospect. Even among those who have to return, some are just as happy, because they are coming back to their old friends and to familiar surroundings and an atmosphere of security.

Joy and sorrow alternate, however, not only in the comings and goings, but also in the staying. The more I explored the wards, the more convinced I became that the vast majority of these patients are satisfied with their lot. In fact, there are an exuberance and a happiness in the air which are hard to find elsewhere. This is almost always true of the moderately retarded and very often true of the severely retarded. As I noticed very early in my dealings with these people, the problems increase in direct ratio to the intelligence level. The brighter a person is, the more capable he is of finding reasons to be unhappy. It is, indeed, no novel statement to say that it takes intelligence to appreciate evil. But I had to live with the retarded before I fully realized that what God denies to the mind, He grants to the heart. Perhaps I should not have been astonished, but I was, when I discovered that less intelligence means more innocence. I already knew that innocence is bliss.

If there is an infinite variety among retarded children, the variations are no less endless in the normal range of humanity. Anyone who walks among men knows that. Among my thousand fellow employees, therefore, I could expect to find all kinds. Many of them impressed me as outstanding people. Some seemed indifferent. And there must be a few who are incompetent. But we can usually presume that most normal people are good, sincere, conscientious, and well intentioned. Even during these early days in my new job, this developed into more than a presumption with me. As I viewed with increasing interest and understanding what was going on, I became convinced that, by and large, my fellow workers were dedicated people.

As I talked with attendants and nurses like Joe Gullo and Dorothy Stark, with supervisors like Bernice McCaffry and Charlie Emerson, with teachers like Helen Bracy and Ed Jennings, and with doctors like Anna Dorgan and Heinz Waller, their interest in and concern for the patients were perfectly obvious. As I watched Dick Keller carrying out his recreation program, as I saw Evelyn MacLaren applying occupational therapy, as I heard Erma Brockhuizen interviewing boarding home girls, their diligence and devotion were clearly evident.

In these first few weeks much of what I discovered about the patients was a revelation to me. Most of what I observed about the personnel was an inspiration. A few of the incidents were a shock.

I was in for another one.

In feeling my way through the intricacies of the institutional setup, I leaned heavily on the guiding hands of two people in particular, Mrs. Cutting, the Chief Supervising Nurse, in charge of Ward (or Nursing) Service, and the Director, Dr. Henne.

Mrs. Cutting was very gracious in helping me arrange my program and in acquainting me with the proper manner of implementing it. Since every program here necessarily requires the assistance of the ward personnel above all others, her advice was invaluable.

As Director, Dr. Henne is the immediate superior of the Chaplain. His patience and kindness in indoctrinating me in the policies of the institution and of the state department and in advising me in my problems and difficulties during those first months were a priceless source of encouragement to me. He was keenly aware of my need for clinical training and deft and adroit in supplying for its absence.

Consequently, it was not unusual to find me in his office at the Front. One morning in mid-August I knocked at his door, prepared to discuss my current problem with him. Instead, he discussed his current problem with me.

Every leader has his share of them. I was soon convinced that no one has more of them than the Director of a State School. He is involved directly or indirectly with every phase and facet of its manifold functions. He is responsible to a formidable array of state officials for an imposing army of employees, a vast multitude of patients, and a forbidding conglomeration of details.

He is also responsible to the members of society, who are often uninformed, skeptical, demanding, and sometimes suspicious, ungrateful, and downright rebellious.

At the moment, he was furious. In his effort to provide me with a cordial welcome, his fury at first remained concealed. But as soon as I stated my problem, it was displayed in all its force.

I had been wondering what the defined policy was in the matter of disciplining or punishing the patients.

That did it. The valve burst.

"Don't mention those words!"

I was aghast. Had I done something wrong? This usually placid and soft-spoken man was seething.

"Look at this!"

He picked up a copy of a local scandal sheet and handed it to me. The headlines hit me with the force of a bulldozer: ATROCITIES AGAIN DEVELOP AT STATE SCHOOL. BRUTALITY RESUMED. I was speechless, but Dr. Henne was not.

"What is the matter with that man? I have repeatedly invited him to inspect this place. He has come and conferred with me many times. And he persists in printing this rubbish. Look at it!"

I was. With unbelieving eyes, I was scanning the sensational story of the "atrocities" that were being perpetrated all around me.

The writer was apparently one of those self-styled redeemers of mankind, a crusader with a destiny to fulfill, with an inviolable commission to clean up every mess he can uncover. Apparently he was also endowed with some special sixth sense for uncovering messes that do not even exist, and that was what he was doing now, according to Dr. Henne. He had already "reformed" the institution by means of his "revelations" in a previous issue. Now the place needed a "cleaning out" again.

"Just look at it! What do you think we should do?"

I could tell from the overwhelming indignation gripping the doctor that the question with which I had come to his office was not going to be answered. And I could tell him that his question was not going to be answered, either—at least, not by me at that time. I was still speechless, for one thing. More than that, I had formed no opinion. But the doctor wanted one.

"What would you do?"

"I don't know," I said. "I'm shocked just by the headline. But I really don't know what he's getting at from the brief glance I've given this. I'd have to read it over thoroughly before I could venture an opinion."

"By all means. Take it along. Read it over. Let me know what you think."

I lost no time in reading it over: the feature article, an editorial, and a letter to the editor. The feature article told the "documented" story of a helpless little girl who was unmercifully beaten by one of our attendants and called for an official investigation. It also mentioned much worse happenings of yore which, however, had all been rectified and atoned for as a result of the newspaper's previous campaign. The article also generously admitted that other institutions had been reformed in the same way.

The editorial was a flag-waving statement of policy: We shall correct evil anywhere we find it, no matter what it may cost. Look what we have already done at the State School, etc.

But the letter to the editor really took the cake. It recounted very solemnly how we broke the arms and legs of male patients—and *then* sent them down in dirty dungeons to prepare vegetables!

I looked at the date on the paper. Could it be? Yes, it was the current issue. But surely they must be getting their material from the Dark Ages! Or maybe they have a ghost-writer who's really a ghost. Certainly no one could actually believe that stuff.

"They do, though; they do believe it. People get all excited. They write the governor and send telegrams to the commissioner and call me on the phone and send demanding letters and—"

"But, Dr. Henne, it's ridiculous. I just called to tell you what I would do. We can discuss it later, but I thought you would like to know my opinion in the meantime. That's why I phoned."

"Yes, of course. I'm sorry this thing gets me so upset. I do want your opinion. What would you do?"

"Nothing."

"*Nothing?* But, Father, have you read those accusations? Do you realize—"

"I realize just one thing: such preposterous accusations don't deserve recognition. They aren't true, are they?"

"Of course not, but not all of our employees are perfect. Some of them do make mistakes."

"But not the mistake of beating up helpless little girls and breaking the limbs of defenseless boys."

"No, I hope not."

"Then, in my opinion, such ignorant charges deserve only to be ignored."

I was sure the Director wasn't convinced. I was, however. I was convinced that the newspaper's crusade was a

lot of balderdash. I was still new on the scene, but I did not
have that monstrous set of keys for nothing. I had been
using them, letting myself in and out of every nook and
corner—uninvited and unannounced, but not unwanted. I
felt welcome everywhere I went. And I had never seen
anyone rushing to hide anything—except perhaps a mag-
azine or a deck of cards. And while I do not approve of
loafing on the job, I know there is bound to be some wherever there are men working. I also know that there are
other mistakes made—in this institution, as well as everywhere else. But I did not consider that anything I had seen
or heard about was atrocious or brutal.

I knew that none of our vegetables was prepared in any
dungeon—let alone a *dirty* dungeon. I had not come across
a single patient with a broken bone of any kind in almost
two months. And I honestly had not seen one child who
looked beaten up—let alone unmercifully.

Even though I probably had not discovered every possible hiding place, I also knew that they were not conceal-
ing the "battered up" patients from me. I had already
interviewed scores of patients for one reason or another,
and no matter whom I requested to see, they were always
able to produce the desired boy or girl. Furthermore, all
my attendance lists checked out perfectly.

It would be unrealistic, indeed, if I tried to persuade
myself that there was no room for improvement in the
State Schools. And surely I had come here with an open
mind. In fact, I had been skeptical. I remembered wondering what the place would be like. And to myself I had used
words like "sinister" and "disagreeable" and "weird." I
had already offered some constructive criticism to Mrs.

Cutting and made some suggestions to Dr. Stevenson. I could even conceive of an attendant or some other employee slapping a patient or shaking him or otherwise sternly disciplining him. That was why I had gone to the Director's office that morning—to find out just what the policy was on correction and punishment, because I could already perceive that some of the brighter patients could be troublesome enough to ask for it. And, of course, I knew that there must be some employees who might reach the breaking point and give it to them.

Well, I found out what the policy was—the same as it was in any other school. Every possible kind of corporal punishment was absolutely forbidden. And I can still imagine a slight infraction of that rule now and then, being aware as I am of some of the weaknesses of human nature.

But brutality and atrocities? No! I was convinced. And I was sure my conviction was unbiased. Nevertheless, I wanted to substantiate that conviction even further. As I continued making acquaintances, interviewing patients, and visiting one area after the other, I kept my eyes open even wider and my ear even closer to the ground. At times I felt like a detective. But, try as I would, I could not detect a single atrocity. No matter where I searched, I could find no evidence of brutality.

The most solid proof for my argument came from the patients themselves. Like all clergymen, the Chaplain in an institution is also considered a sort of all-round troubleshooter. And I had heard complaints from both employees and patients. Surely, if any of these boys and girls were being beaten up, one of them would have let the fact slip by this time. I even provided opportunities for them to reveal any "torture tactics." I especially left the way wide open for Ted, my houseboy, to cue me in on any horrors that were being perpetrated.

Nothing.

That was it—nothing! That was the trouble—stressing the *negative*. We have to accentuate the *positive*. We have to let people know what does go on in these places. Why should we be on the defensive all the time? Denying the claims of the scandal sheet would be a waste of time. The accusations are too childish to argue with. But we do not have to argue. All we have to do is state the facts—without any reference to our accusers.

And that is what I did. I stated the facts as I saw them. I wrote an article describing my impressions as the new Chaplain at the State School. I endeavored to be as fair and square as I could. When I finished it, I took it up Front—to Dr. Henne.

He liked it, and he liked the approach. He agreed that the best way to fight back is not to fight at all, but just to make a display of arms. He agreed that we should make every effort to present a good image. Of course, I was not convincing him of the need for good public relations. That was already an important part of his job.

When I read my article in the newspaper, I realized that it was an important part of my job, too.

All of us are engaged in the conflict on this battlefield— that, I had discovered earlier. Now I knew that we had to join forces also in a *cold* war.

XII

PARENTS ARE PEOPLE, TOO

PUBLIC relations in the State School nowhere acquire greater importance than when we are dealing with the parents of patients. Naturally, they are the people in the community whose concern in the affairs of the institution is most vital. The number of consultations I was having with parents left no doubt in my mind about that. I could see why the state regulations for Chaplains required them to be present on Saturdays and Sundays, since those were the days when most parents were able to visit their children. They often wanted to visit the Chaplain, too.

Bringing a retarded child into the world is one of the most bitter experiences a parent can have. Bringing him to an institution is almost as bitter for the majority of them. Perhaps the most common of all these parents' miseries is a guilt complex, which often reaches its zenith at the time of institutionalization. For many, this makes an early session with the Chaplain imperative.

I had not had many of these sessions before it became

obvious that the comings and goings and stayings of the patients wrought a far greater hardship on the parents than on their children. Even a profoundly retarded child will have great difficulty at times adjusting to his new mode of life, but sometimes this is more a physiological problem than an emotional one. However, it is a rare mother and father who do not have an even more profound adjustment to make than that of their child.

Typical parents in this regard were Jennie and Sam. I had known them for five or six years and had come to look on them as the ideal husband and wife and model parents. Both of them were conscientious, level-headed, likable people. Their first child was severely retarded and a constant care. Patsy got that constant care from his parents for nine years.

In the meantime, however, three other babies—among them a set of twins—had come along. As little Patsy increased in size, so did the family problems he was creating. Jennie and Sam were at their wit's end. It was becoming an impossibility to give both Patsy and the other children the care they needed. But what to do? Patsy had always been considered a special trust, and despite his inability to understand, he was dearly loved by his parents. Even the thought of an institution seemed a crime to Sam and his wife. But they loved their other children, too. Was it fair to make them bear the encumbrance caused by their brother's condition? Were they even being fair to themselves? Did God Himself want things that way?

Who of us is able to answer questions like these for himself? Sam and Jennie were not, so they decided to pay me a visit. Of course, they wanted to know about the institution. But most of all, they wanted to know about themselves. Would they be doing the right thing? They had dozens of questions, but they knew that the answer to the ultimate question had to come from themselves. No one else can make decisions for us, but the opinions of qualified people can often ease the pain involved in the making of them.

As a priest, a friend, and now a Chaplain of the retarded, I was deemed by Jennie and Sam qualified to help. As priest and Chaplain, I was able to provide them with two kinds of considerations: moral and institutional. But any good friend would have been qualified to supply the inescapable practical opinion: inescapable.

I could not see that there was much choice. To keep the child at home any longer was next to impossible. Day care or day school was out of the question, too, because Patsy was not educable, was scarcely trainable, and required constant supervision. And I knew that Jennie and Sam could not afford a private boarding home. They knew all these things, too, but since their opinions were also their fears, they needed to have them confirmed by a friend, substantiated by a Chaplain, and approved by a priest. Even though they had already received much medical and psychiatric advice, I thought they should also have the opinion of one of our own physicians. They gladly accepted an appointment with Dr. Stevenson.

For some time the decision to institutionalize their child had seemed inescapable to Jennie and Sam. But with such powerful emotions involved, who would dare to say that his own conclusion was the right one, that it was *really* the only way out? After consultation, people in such circumstances may not actually feel much better about the decision they know they have to make, but they are intellectually more solidly established. Nevertheless, most of us conclude such interviews by saying, as Sam and his wife did, "We *feel* so much better about it now."

But Sam and his wife did not feel very good the day they brought their child to be admitted. What loving parent does? Perhaps those who have never had a retarded child to love cannot understand that the ties of affection between parents and their handicapped children are often exceptionally strong. Even severely retarded children understand it at times, though. I am not sure little Patsy understood it, but his parents did. It broke their hearts to turn homeward without him. It would be the first time in nine years that he was absent from their home.

Patsy's usual reaction to almost anything was a scream. This had been the source of many of the difficulties at home, especially with the other children. Since this reaction continued at the school, it was difficult to determine whether the boy was adjusting well or not—at least during the first few days. At the end of a week it became obvious that he was not adjusting at all.

His parents had not adjusted either. At the end of the first week they could not bear the separation any longer. So they headed for the School. Had I known they were coming so soon, I might have advised against such a premature visit.

But I didn't know it—until I walked into the lobby of the Boys' Hospital on my routine rounds. Even as I started up the steps to the building, I recognized Patsy's familiar scream. This day it was incessant. Inside, I found the three of them, and it was difficult to decide who was the most uncontrollable. Jennie and Sam, streaming with tears, were absolutely unable to make contact with their constantly screaming son. The efforts of everyone else failed as well. The attendant tried; the ward physician tried; the supervisor tried; I tried—all to no avail. Patsy had to be taken, screaming and disconsolate, back to the admission ward.

Jennie and Sam were plunged in grief and overwhelmed with self-accusation. They were sure they had done the wrong thing.

They had. They had made a dreadful mistake—but a very natural one. They came to see their boy too soon. But how could they know that this is such an unpredictable factor? Dr. Farnham and I talked with them for an hour. They were concerned about Patsy's loss of weight. The doctor explained that this often happens until a new admission becomes accustomed to institutional cooking. Both of us assured them that their early visit was their only mistake. We were sure the boy would be much better adjusted by the time of their next visit. But the parents of Patsy were just as disconsolate as their son when they departed that Sunday afternoon.

Sam and his wife were sensible people, not the kind who float around on a cloud of sentimentality. But they had a good share of the emotions which God wisely puts into parental hearts. It is understandable that those hearts were broken. But they had no intention of just pining away in unavailing grief. On the way home, despite their heartache, they tried to analyze the situation in the light of the discussion with Dr. Farnham and me. They firmly determined that they were going to try to be practical about the whole thing.

They were. The very next day six cans of a popular brand of pork and beans arrived at Dr. Farnham's office. They were delivered by a friend of Jennie and Sam's, who was coming to visit her son. Dr. Farnham phoned to tell me about it. He read the note that came with the cans:

"On the way home yesterday, my husband and I recalled how fond our Patsy is of canned pork and beans. We thought maybe this little contribution would help to bridge the gap between our table and yours. We hope it is all right to do this."

It was more than all right. It was an inspiration. Everyday Patsy was served some of the canned beans along with the regular institution food. Gradually the beans disappeared, and by that time the rest of the food was disappearing, too—via Patsy.

About two weeks elapsed before I saw the boy again. He was sitting quietly by the doorway to the admission ward one day as I entered. Almost without thinking, I held out my hand and said, "Hello, Patsy." If I had stopped to think, I would have approached him much more cautiously, because an extended hand had always been a sure scream trigger. But Patsy's reaction that day startled me much more than a scream: he stood up, took my hand, and came to me. Thank God! He was over the hump.

The next time I saw Patsy's parents they were just as overcome with joy as they had been overwhelmed with grief on the previous occasion. They had taken their son out for a ride, stopped for an ice-cream cone, and returned him to the ward—and the whole process had been completely screamless. Nor had Patsy said a word to his mother and father. He never will. But his message got through to them. Jennie and Sam didn't have to say a word to me either. When I saw their smiling faces I got the same message—and with almost as great a thrill as the day their little boy took my hand.

XIII

IN HIGH GEAR

PATIENTS, personnel, parents—all of them were teaching me fast and furiously. I kept thinking of the tons of clinical training which the Bishop had predicted would come with the job. In those first months of my tenure I had indeed learned a lot.

However, I had not come here to *learn,* really. I had come to *teach.* But it is a reciprocal action—like saving souls. I am here primarily to save souls—and, by that very act, to save my own. The salvation of souls is accomplished, not only by praying and preaching, but also by teaching. So I had better get busy and start teaching.

That was the thought that had been haunting me for some time. But, like patients and parents, I had to get adjusted, too. There would be no use in starting a catechetical program until after Labor Day, because summer activities, especially vacations, would not be compatible to a rigid class schedule.

I was disturbed to realize that in the course of my own

bewildering learning process, Labor Day had already come and gone, and I had not made the slightest move in the direction of establishing a program of religious instruction.

It was not only my involvement in all these other unfamiliar facets of institutional adjustment that delayed the development of the catechetical program. It was my absolute perplexity with the prospect. The alarm which overwhelmed me kept expressing itself in the simple question, "Where do I begin?"

At the beginning. I finally decided that was the only answer: I had to start from scratch. The reason is not hard to understand. Before the days of the resident Chaplain, religious instructions in State Schools were of necessity limited to preparation for First Communion and Confirmation. Priests responsible for the care of the school, in addition to their parochial burdens, had all they could do to provide for the essential ministrations to these patients. The first resident Chaplain had a whole new phase of the ministry to develop. He had only recently arrived at the task of experimenting with a complete catechetical program when I arrived to take over. And I found it impossible to take up where he had left off—mostly because his program had been experimental and incomplete. Another difficulty was posed by the great dearth, at that time, of instructional material for the retarded.

In the seminary some of our subjects had been taught in cycle courses. Students on three or four different levels attended the same class, starting the course at whatever cycle it happened to be when they arrived at the first of those levels. But that would be ridiculous. You cannot do that with the retarded.

Why not? I have to be sure that at least all the educable boys and girls are at least exposed to at least the essentials of the complete course of Christian doctrine. That means more than 500 of them—at least. Besides, I have to have a First Communion class, a Confirmation class, an altar boy class. Lord, help me! He has to help me, because otherwise I would be attempting an impossible task. Of course, I know I can depend on His help, because it is really *His* program.

What I did not know was how many other persons I could depend on for help. I soon found out when I discovered how complicated it is to set up a 3-year cycle course for more than 500 patients in one of the State Schools for the mentally retarded. The only questions I had to answer were, who is to be instructed, what are they to be taught, where are the classes to be held, when, and how?

I started making the rounds: Protestant Chaplain, Director of Education, Chief Supervising Nurse, supervisors, attendants, teachers. Everyone pitched in with advice, ideas, suggestions, and offers of help. After much praying, weighing, and surveying, a concrete program finally materialized: all the patients who are able to go to church will attend the classes; the cycle will start with the Commandments, continue with the Sacraments, and conclude with the Creed; classes will be conducted in the Assembly Hall; all the boys will come every Thursday night, all the girls every Saturday afternoon.

It all sounds so simple. But when a class has to be sandwiched in between a dozen other programs held in the same place for 250 people engaged in a score of other activities on 15 different wards, involved with half a dozen various departments, under the supervision of innumerable employees—it is not simple.

In fact, there just is not anything simple about a class of 250, to begin with. The very idea is fantastic. Who would be so bold and brash as even to toy with the idea? No one but a neophyte Chaplain, who felt he had no alternative. And even he would not dare attempt it with normal children. Three months earlier the thought of a class of 250 retardates would have completely appalled me.

But by the middle of October it was a pleasant reality. Visually, it was an anomaly. Walking into the hall, you would see little boys, teen-agers, and old men in a single class. But, after all, why couldn't I teach the same physical variety of people on Thursday that I preach to on Sunday? The intellectual variation is not nearly so wide. Every IQ is under 75, and most of them are over 30—a span of only 45. Regardless of appearances, the top mental age is about 10. Of course, an old lady with a mental age of 10 is not just like a teen-age girl on the same intellectual level. But, especially from the spiritual standpoint, these children of God are always children—the young at heart. And that is what I have to appeal to most of all in these classes: the heart.

I started with the one thing that goes right to the heart of all of us, whether we are intellectual giants or mental dwarfs: music. The girls' choir had taught me that retardates were no exception to the appeal of its charms. Both boys and girls, from youngest to oldest, were captivated by "The Ten Commandments Song." They learned the words and music in no time, and they were as quiet and attentive as church mice in the process.

Of course, rattling off lyrics and melodies does not mean comprehension of the doctrines contained therein. It took a whole year to detail the material embraced by that one song. I was sure that many of the pupils were not acquiring very much theology, but at least most of them were able to verbalize the Commandments of God. I also began to suspect that many were comprehending more than they would ever be able to make an account of. In any case, I was sure that no harm was being done. If even the littlest minds progressed even the slightest bit in the love of God, it was all to the good. If nothing more could be said, many who had never known anything about God's Law were now learning something about it. Any doubts I had about the validity of the procedure were soon reduced to a minimum.

There was no doubt at all that everybody was learning at least one thing: music. They just seemed to gobble it up. They had mastered the whole "Commandments Song" long before we finished the doctrinal consideration of even the First Commandment. And we could not just go on singing that one selection. So we went on learning one after the other. The same record happens to contain a song for each of the seven Sacraments, too. By the time all the doctrine had been wrung out of the first song, the musical repertoire of the catechism classes had increased to eight. We had a head start on the cycle for the following year.

Week after week, Sarah and Janet set up the hall for classes. Week after week, supervisors and attendants gathered the patients together and escorted them to the sessions.

Week after week, Ted hooked up the record player and the PA system. The religious instruction program was in high gear.

It was not the ideal arrangement by any means. Retardates should be taught in very small groups. But it was the only way to take up the slack. In three years I could be sure that everyone had in some way been through a course of instruction. Then it would be possible to dispense with classes for the older people and concentrate on the younger ones in small groups. In the meantime, everyone was learning something: some little prayers, some simple doctrines, some basic principles—and some songs!

Why not some hymns? The Church stressed strongly the desirability of congregational singing—and praying. Of course, I could not expect the retarded to learn the Latin responses of the Mass. But if they could sing songs, they could sing hymns. I knew the choir girls could. Why not the rest of them?

In no time the voices of the choir girls were being joined by 500 others. My congregation had learned its first hymn. It was only the beginning. For the choir girls it was the beginning of the end. But they had a job to do before the choir would come to its end. They were the first ones to learn each new hymn. Stan Kardys, our music teacher, began spending all his rehearsal time in teaching the girls the traditional hymns used for congregational singing. Then the girls were scattered throughout the rest of the congregation as the other boys and girls began to learn words and music. Each week the volume grew until at last the rafters were ringing for joy.

If songs, why not hymns; if English hymns, why not

Latin hymns? The choir girls already knew the two Benediction hymns in Latin. If hymns, why not prayers? Maybe
they could learn some of the Latin Mass responses.

And so they could. It was amazing. The weekly catechism classes became a workshop for doctrine, morals,
music, language, and liturgy. What at first seemed an impossible arrangement became a bonanza. The unbelievable number of pupils in these two classes were so engrossed in their new adventures that they did not have
time to misbehave. And their teacher was so entranced
with it all that he forgot to worry about the question of
discipline. The more he taught, the more he learned.

The Assembly Hall on Sunday mornings was gradually
acquiring the atmosphere of a church. After a few months
of the Thursday night and Saturday afternoon sessions
the whole congregation was singing and praying together
like choir monks. The choir *girls* had lost their identity,
but the dying seed had borne abundant fruit. The only
discordant note was not vocal, but instrumental. The ac-
companiment still came from a piano. And the visual fea-
tures were little redolent of the house of God. However,
the Church is the people, not the edifice; it is the people
praying and singing and worshiping God together, not the
beauty of the altar or the richness of the musical instru-
ment.

The material elements do help, though, because we are
composite beings. Unlike angels, we find it difficult to comprehend and appreciate and savor that which is exclusively spiritual. We need material crutches, like Christian
symbols and liturgical colors and ecclesiastical architecture
and church organs.

Finally the day came when the Assembly Hall was really transformed, when it became the nearest thing to a church you could ever expect of an assembly hall. That was the day the first note reverberated through the new convertible sanctuary from the voice box of the long-awaited electronic organ.

The boys and girls were entranced. The beautiful music, the colorful symbols, the lovely pictures, the stately altar, the Oriental carpets gave many of them their first real taste of Heaven. I do not think any of them ever realized how much more heavenly their voices made it.

XIV

OUTSIDE IN

MY orientation took much more than a day—or even a year
—of course, but it is strange how different things seem
after we get used to them. In six months I was using all
the local expressions as though I had been born with them.
It had become perfectly natural for me to refer to the
institution as the Hill, the Administration Building as the
Front, and the community as the Outside.

In six months I could find my way around as though I
had drawn the plans for the place. No longer did everything seem so vast and incomprehensible and frightening.
Hundreds of faces and places, objects, and objectives had
become familiar to me. I was manipulating red tape as
easily as my shoelaces and writing requisitions like post-
cards. The learning process was not over by any means.
Is it ever? But I could never again be as green as I had
once been about mental retardation and State Schools.
And I could never unlearn the many wonderful acquaintances I had made.

Among the acquaintances were some members of the
clergy. Before the Chaplaincy had been established, the
parish priests living nearest to institutions like this had
always been responsible for the spiritual care of the residents. Now the responsibility had ceased, but the interest
of these men had not. The village pastor and his curate
knew the State School as well as they knew their parish.
Consequently, the local clergy had been among the earliest
of my acquaintances. Along with Ted, Emma, and Achiel,
they were the first members of "The Club." Not only were
they able to enlighten and encourage me, but they were
also gracious in covering for me, so that I could get a respite from my responsibilities by taking my pass days regularly. Most of all, from the very start, I had always been
a most welcome guest at the rectory downtown, where I
could frequently be found at the dinner table. I was thus
afforded an appropriate refuge from my frustrations.

Outstanding among my frustrations at this time was my
program. It still needed a tremendous amount of development. But at least I had an idea of the direction that development must take. We never know all the answers, but
we have come a long way when we know most of the
questions. It was getting so that I even knew whom to *ask*
most of the questions. I had really begun to feel assimilated
and to know what it was like to be on the inside looking
out.

That was what I was beginning to do more and more—
look out. My first view from the inside out had been
through the eyes of the patients. They often referred to
the way things are on the Outside. And, of course, those
going to and from parole were always talking about the

Outside. I became aware of the view from the outside in when I started my consultation with parents. The scandal sheet incident had forcibly demonstrated to me how inside-out a place can look from the outside and how important it is to have ins and outs from both sides.

I had long been aware of the vital role of our Social Service Department in the matter of ins and outs—from the inside. Now I was learning something about the role as it is played from the outside.

When the order was placed for the electronic organ, it became evident that we would have to make some provision for a voice box. Chaplain Blaisdell, Mr. Rockwood, and I decided that this was the time to do something about the worship facilities. So we designed a huge wooden triptych, which would serve as voice box, altar storage, reredos, and sanctuary all folded up into one. Our Maintenance Department could handle the construction. The question was where to secure the two or three hundred dollars to cover the cost of materials and the artwork.

I had heard of the Sunshine League. I knew it was sponsored by parents who were members of the Association for Retarded Children for the benefit of the patients in the institution. But only now did I learn that this group was providing some $12,000 a year for such things as entertainment, parties, and recreational equipment for our boys and girls. Could we use some of that fund for our convertible sanctuary? As long as it was convertible, yes, because it would be used by all three major faiths and would therefore benefit all the patients.

Our triptych began to materialize from materials provided by the Sunshine League. It was wonderful when we moved in to our new sanctuary that first Sunday and were able to tell the patients that our church was a little more like a real church because of the good friends they had on the Outside.

That was the day we started the special congregational prayers which we say every Sunday for "our friends, relatives, and benefactors." And ever since that day the number included in those prayers has been on the increase, because so much has continued to come from the Outside.

The little chapel in my residence had been established only a couple of years, and because of lack of funds, its furnishings and equipment were mostly loans and hand-me-downs. Sunshine League funds could not be used for such denominational purposes, of course. But maybe there would be other Outsiders who would like to help. I decided to make our needs known.

The benefactors came running. Candlesticks, sanctuary lamp, crucifix, tabernacle, stained-glass windows—all were bought, put in place, and paid for in a matter of months. High school mission units, parish societies, family groups, and individuals rallied to the cause. The response was tremendous.

"Is there anything else you need, Father?" became a regular question. Yes, what we really need is an adequate, honest-to-goodness, full-size chapel—a church. No matter how well equipped a hall is, it is still a hall, and these children need a church. But I dared only to think it in those early days. What I dared to say was: "Yes, we need rosaries, prayer books, medals, crucifixes, statues, and all kinds of religious articles." From the Outside, in they came in such a steady stream that I would never again have to say, "Sorry, I don't have a Bible."

Money, equipment, supplies, and encouragement were not our only needs. Of all things, I discovered that I needed *people*. I could manage a First Communion class of fifteen or twenty. I could handle a group of a dozen altar boys. I could even carry off those king-size catechism classes on Thursday nights and Saturday afternoons. But I could not imagine training eighty patients single-handed for Confirmation. I needed people.

From the Outside, in they came, and they have never stopped coming—catechists, typists, clerical workers. I soon had ten, then twenty. Our volunteer program, which was then in its infancy, was to grow into a giant. After a full-time supervisor was appointed to the job in the person of Pearl Beers, the recruits began to come by the dozen, then in scores, and finally by the hundreds.

My own volunteer program began with those first Confirmation instructors. They were truly a godsend. Four times a week they came to teach and train the boys and girls in small groups. At the end of the preparation period they helped with the rehearsals in the hall and finally acted as sponsors, each for the members of his own little group. The ceremony went like clockwork, but it could never have been that way without our friends from the Outside.

These wonderful people were the nucleus of a group which was to become the mainstay of the catechetical program. They continued with First Communion groups, Infirmary classes, and individual instructions and would one day carry on where the cycle course would leave off. Of all the things that were coming to us from the community, nothing was as precious as the people.

In ever greater numbers they were coming, not only to work, but just to look. Open House, held once a year, was giving everybody an opportunity to see what made us tick. But more and more, individuals and small groups— students, teachers, nurses, doctors, professionals, and just plain people—were coming for tours and talks and tastes of institutional life.

It would be hard to trump up scandals for sensation seekers again. Most of the people on the Outside were finally discovering that most of us on the inside are just people from the Outside in.

XV

NORA

PUBLIC relations were constantly improving. Not only were the members of society visiting and getting acquainted with the institution, but those on the inside were daily becoming more outgoing. Members of the staff were attending more and more meetings in the community and delivering more and more lectures and talks. Increasing numbers of patients were being taken out to sports events, entertainments, and civic projects. Our drum and bugle corps and our Boy and Girl Scouts were making public appearances and being given various kinds of recognition by society. Busloads of our patients were being transported all over the countryside.

I was impressed by the growing give-and-take between the public and the institution. But the growing intake made the deepest impression. All our facilities were heavily overtaxed, since our accommodations were already 40 percent overcrowded. And still they came. Hardly a day passed without at least one new admission. It seemed that all the retardates on the Outside would soon be on the inside. Despite increased efforts toward the discharge and community placement of our boys and girls, despite the regularity of the death toll, our number was constantly increasing. I was sure that there could not be many more left in the community.

I was in for another shock. Only 5 percent of the retarded children in our country are institutionalized. Ninety-five percent of them remain at home. Thank God for that! It is good for them and for us that they do. But if we have only 5 percent of them in our institutions, the total number of retarded Americans must be staggering. And so it is: 6,000,000.

These statistics made me hungry for more. I had noticed several volumes of the annual *Report of the Board of Visitors* among the books in my office. The last pages of each report constituted a statistical summary. Until now these pages had presented nothing more to me than a jumble of figures as I flipped through them. I decided to take a closer look.

In the previous year our patient registration had grown from 3,969 to 4,017. It was an increase of only 48. But during that time, 131 had been discharged, 10 had been transferred out, and 86 had died, while the intake for the same period amounted to 275.

Only 120 of the latter were mine. *Only* 120? I was beginning to talk like my predecessor. Of course, I had not interviewed all 120 of those new admissions, because the *Report of the Board of Visitors* ran from April 1 to March 31, and I had been present for only three-quarters of that time. But I had surely interviewed a lot of them. It was fascinating in a way: to make an estimate of a new admission and then to compare that estimate later with the psychometric report or the future developments on the patient's ward or the information volunteered by members of the family.

Nora Bennet's was an interesting case. Nora was a well-developed girl of twenty-three. She wore glasses perched on the little pug nose mounted in the center of her perfectly round face. You would not believe a face could be so static. I had thought Ted's countenance was expressionless, but he did smile, even laugh, once in a while. Not Nora. I decided that her expression had never changed since the day she was born. Emotionally, the girl seemed to be just as conservative. When it came to speech, Nora was downright miserly.

I had not talked with Nora very long before I determined that all this thriftiness of facial, emotional, and verbal expression was not a result of the severity of her retardation. I judged that she was moderately retarded—perhaps with an IQ of about 45. Strangely enough, I was able to make some estimate of her knowledge despite her "monoverbiage." Nora did not speak in words of one syllable, but in sentences of one word. It was as if she had promised someone never to exceed that limit.

I had been intrigued at first by the immobility of Ted's lips when he spoke. Nevertheless, all his words were clearly formed. And, of course, if you watched closely, you could see that his lips really were moving when he talked, even if ever so slightly. But not Nora's. When you conversed with Nora, there was absolutely no perceptible motion in any part of her. It made even her single words rather difficult to understand.

My first interview with her went like this:

"Hello, Nora."

" 'Lo."

"How are you?"

"Fine."

"Can you tell me how old you are?"

"Twny."

"Twenty?"

"Three."

"Twenty-three?"

"Yes."

"When is your birthday?"

"April."

"April what?"

"Six."

"Can you count for me?"

"One."

"What's next?"

"Two."

"Go ahead."

"Three."

"Keep right on going."

"Four."

I think we got as far as ten when I decided that we could go on like that for hours and that I had better get into the religion department:

"How many gods are there, Nora?"

"One."

"How many Persons in God?"

"Three."

"That's right. Can you name the three Persons for me?"

"Father."

"Yes. Go on, please."

"Son."

"Is that all?"

"Ghost."

"You mean *Holy* Ghost."

"Yes."

"Who is the next Person?"

"All."

"That's all?"

"Yes."

"Who is Mary?"

"Mother."

"Whose mother?"

"Jesus."

"Do you know how Jesus saved us?"

"Died."

"How did He die?"

"Cross."

"What did He do the night before He died?"

"Mass."

"What else?"

"Communion."

"What is Communion?"

"Body."

"Is that all?"

"Blood."

"Whose Body and Blood?"

"Jesus."

And so it went. My unbelieving ears were hearing every answer in the catechism reduced to one word. Strangely enough, every word Nora said was correct. I decided that she was quite capable of going to Mass and receiving the Sacraments, and I marked her admission slip and transfer card accordingly. It was obvious that Nora was retarded and that, like all retardates, she had a personality all her own. It did not occur to me to ask Nora why she had been admitted. When I later discovered the reason, I wondered how she would have put it in one word. The information came to me in many more words than one.

It was the following Saturday afternoon. I had all but forgotten about Nora, when a mousy little middle-aged man appeared at my office. He was weeping, and he wanted me to help him. I said I would be glad to do what I could, but I wondered who he was.

"Tom. I'm Tom Bennet."

"Oh, yes. I've already talked with your daughter."

"My wife, Father. Nora's my wife. And that's why I've come to see you. Please help me get her out of here, Father; I need her."

I could not have been more astonished if he had told me that Nora was the Queen of Mesopotamia. I reached for her index card as my visitor continued pleading for my help. Sure enough, she was married. I had never noticed the notation of her maiden name on the card. But there it was—"née Sczylich," in black and white.

"It's so lonesome without her, Father," Tom was saying through his tears. "They should never put her here, Father. It isn't fair."

I was wondering who had put her here.

"The judge, Father, the judge, but it wasn't her fault. She couldn't help it."

Couldn't help what?

"Because the baby died."

My gosh, did she have a baby?

"No, Father, it wasn't our baby. It was somebody else's."

What in the world happened?

"It burned to death, Father, when Nora was baby-sittin'."

In a flash I knew who Nora was. Like everyone else in the area, I had read her story in the newspaper. It was a sad tale. Maybe that was why the girl was so expressionless. The poor thing would probably never recover from the experience.

She had been baby-sitting when the house caught fire. In her fright, Nora had fled, leaving the infant behind in his crib. Her tragic story was that simple. And the tragedy could just as simply have been avoided. Nora could not help it because she lacked the sense of responsibility to pick up that child and take him with her. But it should have been obvious to the people who hired her. They had given the burden of supervision to someone who was scarcely able to care for herself without constant supervision. Tom was right; it was not her fault; she could not help it.

And I could not help him, either—at least not the way he wanted me to. It was evident that Tom was only slightly more capable than his wife. He surely was not able to provide the supervision she would need out in society. Nora had to have the protection provided by the school. That is difficult to explain to anyone who is emotionally upset.

It is doubly difficult when the person is as dull as Tom seemed to be.

However, I made every effort to enlighten and console him. But I do not think Tom ever really understood. I know he was never really consoled. He came to see Nora every Saturday. And he always stopped to see me. It only lasted a few months. One Saturday he failed to appear. Instead, his death notice appeared in that night's paper. He had died of a heart attack.

It was my duty to inform Nora of this new tragedy. I do not think she really understood. But it was difficult to determine. Without the slightest expression, she said, "Tom."

"Yes," I answered, "I'm very sorry, Nora."

She did not cry. She did not move. She simply said, "Oh."

XVI

PERSONALITY KIDS

NORA BENNET was only one of the 275 patients who came to live with us that year. She was not just a statistic, because like every other patient here, Nora had a personality all her own. I came to realize that more and more as I interviewed the new admissions and as I became better acquainted with the established residents. Despite some occasionally startling similarities and regardless of the severity of their retardation, every one of these patients is an individual person.

The statistical summary in the back of each annual *Report of the Board of Visitors* does not deny this fact, to be sure; but figures always have a cold, impersonal way of lumping people together, which certainly does not present a very vivid picture of their individual personalities. Nevertheless, I found myself fascinated by the statistics—and a little overwhelmed. The comings and goings of the patients were listed according to age, mental status, clinical diagnosis, origin, and destination. There was even a compilation of the causes of death and of certain medications used. Every employee position was listed, whether filled or vacant. And, of course, there was a financial report. Nothing is colder than a financial report, although I could not help being impressed by the total cost of operation for the previous year. But then, a figure like 6,000,000 is always impressive. Other figures were impressive, too—like the one which indicated that 384 of our boys and girls had been placed out in the community during that year. Even the list of employees, comprising 133 diverse jobs, was interesting.

However, there is nothing as fascinating as the people behind the lists and figures. The personalities, even of retarded people, can color the background and change the atmosphere and identify the locale. Indeed I soon found myself thinking not only of Mrs. Moorehead's Service, Dr. Kellow's Office, and Mr. Burm's Trucks, but also of Jimmy's Room, Mary's Ward, and Dick's Day.

The third Thursday of the month became Dick's Day for class. The class is held in the Male Infirmary, and Dick is only one of many crippled boys present. But Dick is the one who changes the whole atmosphere of the class. He is thirty-one years old and has spent all but seven of those years here—in a wheelchair. He is no less crippled than most of the other boys, but less retarded than a lot of them. In fact, he is one of the brightest patients in the institution. It is no wonder that he stands out in the religion class, since he comprehends almost every point which is made. He is even able to cooperate by *not* answering questions, so the other fellows will have a chance. The questions he asks are also as remarkable as the ones he can answer.

Dick is a tall, lanky boy with a ready smile. Despite his own handicaps, he keeps very busy helping the other boys. He is not able to manipulate his own wheelchair or to get in and out of it by himself, and yet he manages to assert considerable influence on his ward. That is to be expected, I suppose, of an outgoing person of Dick's caliber.

On the very same ward is Tony, who is half as tall, twice as agile, and a third as bright as Dick. Yet Tony, in his own way, is another outstanding personality. Short, stubby, and ambulatory, Tony is scarcely able to talk; but he understands, and he has an almost perpetual smile. A little younger than Dick, he has been here only a few years and has already established himself as a one-man reception committee. The minute I enter the ward, I know a pair of arms will be thrown around my hips—that's as high as Tony can reach. Nobody understands what he says on such an occasion, but we all know it means welcome. And he seems to understand when his friends call him Lover-boy.

Mary's Ward is officially known as PT, which stands for physiotherapy. It houses both boys and girls of preteen age who have serious physical handicaps and can probably benefit from physiotherapy treatment, surgery, or mechanical aids.

Mary looks perfectly normal. In fact, she is a beautiful child of eight, with an infectious smile. She was admitted when she was a year old. Unable to walk, Mary spends all her time in bed or on a stretcher. More often than not, her legs are in casts as a result of a series of operations. She definitely has the intelligence to assess her plight, but she never utters a complaint. On the contrary, for a child, she has an uncanny ability to deflect attention away from herself by displaying an uncommon interest in her visitor and the things around her. Her coy smile usually means "Did you bring me something?" And no matter how small the present may be, the reward to the giver is always generous, because Mary treats him like the world's outstanding philanthropist.

Jimmy's Room is in the Children's Building, where all the patients are under five. Jimmy is a fragile little boy of four with big brilliant black eyes. Like Mary, he has never walked. But there is no hope for Jimmy, because he has brittle bones, and his crooked little legs could never support him. Just a little wrong move can cause a fracture, so Jimmy will probably never get beyond the bars of his crib —not physically. Yet, even at the age of four, the sparkling personality of this tiny boy is radiating far beyond its confines. At first I could hear him call my name as soon as I entered the building. Now I sometimes hear it as I pass the window. Always on the lookout for his friends, this inquisitive little fellow never misses a trick. And his own best trick is making friends. He has never missed making one out of every person who has ever seen him. And if any of his friends get depressed, all they have to do for a lift is make a stop in Jimmy's Room.

As days grew into weeks and weeks into months, the people around me were helping me grow, too. By the end of my first year as Chaplain of the State School, I could sense a dramatic change in my whole frame of mind. My bewilderment and numbness, my fears and misgivings, my shock and wonderment—had all but dissolved. Even my lack of knowledge and experience had been substantially repaired. Because of personalities like Dick and Tony, Mary and Jimmy, my whole outlook was entirely different.

Friends were still cautiously asking, "Don't you get depressed?" All I could answer was, "No, thank God, I don't." And I really thanked God over and over for that favor, because it would have to be depressing without His support, and if it were depressing, it would be an impossible task. Sometimes one of my inquirers would respond with, "Oh, I suppose you do get hardened to it after a while." And again, I would have to answer, "No, thank God, you don't get hardened to it," because hardness would surely not be a desirable quality in those who work with these children. What happens to us is difficult to explain, if not entirely inexplicable, without attributing it to God's help and to the personalities of the patients themselves.

I often think, for example, of someone like Harry, who is probably one of the oldest hydrocephalics in existence. At the age of twenty-four, he has a head that would more than fill a bushel basket. Anyone seeing him for the first time has to be shocked. I was. I could not believe my eyes. Nor could I believe my ears. For Harry can carry on a fairly coherent conversation. He can also sing a couple of songs. He is one of the friendliest and most cheerful of people. I always stop to chat with Harry and give him a holy picture when I am on his ward. And somehow I never notice the astounding size of his head anymore. I guess it is dwarfed by his personality.

Irene is another one. Her body is so deformed that a special carriage had to be designed to accommodate her unbelievable shape, which is continually contorted even further by her extreme spasticity. Because she is so spastic, she is unable to speak; yet she is able to comprehend and to convey her thoughts to others. And she is able to smile the biggest smile you have ever seen. Whenever I see Irene now, that smile seems to show more than anything else. You might expect to be repelled by someone with the multiple handicaps she has—or at least to be so overcome with pity that it would be unbearable. But somehow that does not happen. Everyone—patients and employees alike—loves Irene. Her personality breaks through all her disabilities and makes her attractive, rather than repellent.

There is another patient here by the name of Claude. His appearance is the kind that prompts people to say, "I wouldn't want to meet him on the street at night." He is very dull and slow to respond. He looks for all the world like a thug. But Claude takes care of Donald with an almost tender devotion.

Donald, a fellow patient of Claude's, is so crippled and so violently spastic that he has to be strapped into a contraption that looks like a mobile coffin. Donald is much brighter than Claude but, because of lack of motor control, can speak only with the greatest of difficulty. Yet these two manage to communicate with each other, and their relationship is an inspiration.

One of the most common sights around here is a combination like Claude and Donald. Everywhere you see those who are only slightly more capable extending a helping hand to the less fortunate. Girls not able to tie a bow in their own apron strings change the beds of the helpless; boys hardly capable of cutting themselves a slice of bread feed those less capable; cripples scarcely ambulatory themselves push others in their wheelchairs.

That sort of thing does not repel and depress. It attracts and inspires. Surely, they are not just statistics—these kids are personalities.

XVII

~~~~~

THE SPICE OF LIFE

PERSONALITIES never develop in a vacuum. People are social beings who start off with a set of individual characteristics which are chiseled, molded, sharpened, and softened by the varying pressures of their environment until they end up with a fusion of unique peculiarities, which we call a personality. The most decisive pressures in the environment of people are exerted by other people. Every personality reflects facets of other personalities to which it has been exposed. This fact is evident in the lives of the retarded, too. If you look closely, you can detect the differences in the "personnelities" reflected in the patients. This is especially true of the very young and of those who have spent most of their lives in the institution. Before long I was able to see the attitudes of attendants reflected in the actions of patients. No matter what church a ward Charge belongs to, if he is a religious man, the boys on his ward will invariably be diligent in the practice of their religion. If a head nurse is neat and tidy, her girls will usually be the same.

Although the personalities of those around us have the most vital influence on the growth of our own, there are also many other factors in our environment which conspire to shape each unique human composite. Only the most naïve or the most stubborn person will deny the premise that people are decisively influenced by what they read and see, by what they hear and where they go, even by what they eat and what sicknesses they have. It is a proved fact that a particular diet deficiency and certain diseases in either mother or child can cause mental retardation. To a lesser degree, many other environmental elements affect the personalities of retarded, as well as normal, people.

It is interesting to observe this interplay of people and things on the development of the human personality. For those working in an institution where the objective is not only the care, but especially the training, education, and habilitation of the mentally retarded, it is more than interesting. It is a solemn responsibility. Such people are charged with the task of providing the kind of environment that will exert the best possible influence on the development of the patients' personalities.

This very necessary project begins with the screening of applicants for the 133 employee positions authorized by the Department of Mental Hygiene for this institution. The original selection of personnel will have a most important bearing on the final collection of personalities. Their background, previous training, and present attitude —all are basic determinants of the desired effect. In addition, the integration of new employees into the institutional system and their in-service training play a vital role in fitting them for the successful accomplishment of their tremendous task.

Employees' Orientation Course, Case Studies in Supervision, Standard Course for Attendants, Work Simplification, Ward Activity Training, Fundamentals of Supervision, In-Service Nurse's Training—the terms themselves indicate the emphasis that is placed on the molding of our personnel for the parts they must play in the molding of personalities. Most of these training programs are designed particularly for the members of Ward Service, since theirs is the most constant influence on the patients. Directing the special courses for ward personnel is our charming Instructor of Nursing, Mrs. Frances Green, who does an expert job of training and enlists in her program the aid of various other experts in the institution. However, some of the courses are given to all the employees, and every department has its own proper training program as well, because ward attendants are by no means alone in their job of providing personal habilitation for the patient. In the final analysis, that is the essential commitment of every one of us, although some are involved only indirectly and even remotely.

Physicians, social workers, teachers, occupational therapists, recreation workers—and Chaplains. All these people are in direct contact with our boys and girls. All the people who work in our industries also work side by side with our patients. And every single one of them contributes something—positive or negative—to the formation of their characters.

Retardates are social beings like the rest of us, because they are people. It is good to see the members of our staff proving themselves to be people, too, by treating our patients like people. The schoolroom, the playground, the workshop, the craft area, and all the material objects in their makeups contribute to the formation of the people for whom they are organized. It is gratifying to see the personnel in charge of every project, whether medical, nursing, educational, recreational, therapeutic, or industrial, making the *preponderant* contribution, as social beings; this makes it essentially a people-to-people operation.

But retardates, like the rest of us, are social beings because they are human beings, and they are human beings because they are not only material, but also spiritual, beings. The human personality is situated fundamentally in the human spirit. Therefore, the spiritual factors in our environment, more than anything else, are responsible for personality development, and the preeminent spiritual factor is religion. Of all the *things* that bear upon our proper formation, the most outstanding are the elements of religion. Among all the *people* who influence the end product of human growth, absolute supremacy is held by God.

With this realization, Chaplain Blaisdell and I often discussed the problem of integration—of making the patient's religion an integral part of his daily life. No matter how well we preach on Sunday or how much we teach on Thursday, no matter how profoundly we impress a patient in our interviews or how often we counsel him, our influence as Chaplains is bound to be restricted in time and place. We need the assistance of people in every department, if the spiritual values which we propound are to become part of the everyday life of the patient, and if we want their assistance, we have to ask for it.

We did. With the cooperation of the part-time Jewish Chaplain, the two resident Chaplains compiled a detailed "Guide to the Religious Needs of Patients." A copy was given to every employee. Then the Chaplains conducted a series of meetings—with the doctors, with the department heads, with ward personnel, with the teachers—for the purpose of suggesting the ways and means of integrating the religious program into the daily routine of the institution and of lending support to Chaplaincy projects. The follow-up was carried out by means of periodic bulletins, memos, and schedules issuing from the Chaplains' offices. By these various means—it was hoped—God and the things of God would be kept before the minds of the personnel and in the hearts of the patients. Some people are poor conductors of religion, as some metals are of electricity. Nevertheless, the religious integration program has been an invaluable asset in the spiritual development of our boys and girls. It receives its value from the people between the patients and their Chaplains.

Those people and the projects they conduct for the training, education, and habilitation of our children are as varied and diverse as the personalities that result. I could see that this is what sprinkled their lives with the much needed spice. Such variety is particularly necessary in the lives of the retarded, because their attention span is so short and their interest wanes so quickly. As soon as this thought had crystallized in my mind, I knew that I had to endeavor to provide as much variety as possible in my own program.

Fortunately, this is not difficult, because the Catholic liturgy abounds in variations of all sorts: the change of vestments, colors, and music; the abundance of symbols; the diversity of ceremonies; and the wealth of prayers and pious practices provide an ever-changing mélange for the weary soul. I determined that I would make the fullest possible use of the Church's treasures to enhance for the patients the practice of their religion.

As my second fall season approached, I decided to conduct a special service on the first Sunday evening of each month. Such an arrangement offered the opportunity of having the patients themselves participate actively in ceremonies like the Living Rosary and the May Crowning and also of presenting a series of guest preachers. Added to the panorama of the regular liturgical services as they unfold during the course of the Church year, these pious practices and devotions permit the patients to worship God in numerous ways, which develop the innumerable facets of their spiritual nature and help them realize that the love of God is a many-splendored thing.

I had learned that the retarded take great delight in celebrating. They announce their birthdays weeks in advance and recount the parties with which they are observed for days afterward. They start wishing you a Happy Thanksgiving as soon as Halloween is over, and they eagerly anticipate Christmas for wccks in advance. The wards and the various departments decorate and celebrate on every possible occasion. Each holiday throughout the year is used as a means of enriching the patient's experience and of adding to his enjoyment.

Many of these events have religious origins or at least religious connotations or overtones. The educational, recreational, therapeutic, or social observance very often has a religious parallel; many holidays are also holy days. Halloween is All Saints' Eve; Thanksgiving Day centers on God's goodness; the best Christmas present of all time is God's Son; God wants to be everyone's Valentine. Shrines, little pageants, special ceremonies, and extra church decorations—all are means of celebrating spiritually which delight these children of God. The Chaplains began to make use of every possible occasion to enrich the souls of the patients and to add to their religious experience by capitalizing on the religious celebrations of the Church year, knowing that, for all God's children, variety is the spice of spiritual life, too.

XVIII

GOD'S HOUSE

THE stateliest house in the world is not necessarily a home. It may be a magnificent place of architecture, an outstanding example of interior decorating, and a national showplace, but if nobody lives there, it is not a home. On the other hand, the ugliest shanty, filled with the love of a husband and wife and their children, thereby becomes a home. No one doubts that home is where the heart is.

Something like that can be said about a church, too. The most splendid cathedral is no longer a church when the enemy stables his horses there in wartime. But when the Army Chaplain says Mass on an orange crate in the rear of a truck for his company, that is a church. A home is where a family is gathered together in love of one another. A church is where God's family is gathered together in love of Him. I was aware of that the very first time I said Mass in our dingy Assembly Hall. Since then a considerable transformation had taken place. The organ, the triptych, the liturgical art, new vestments, the congregational singing and praying—all of these contributed to the development of ecclesiastical atmosphere.

But all the accidentals in the world cannot change the fundamentals. The orange crate does not become a shiny block of marble because it is used as an altar. The shanty does not turn into a garden bungalow because its inhabitants honestly call it home. And there are many points of departure in the comparison of an assembly hall to a church—no matter how much ecclesiastical ingenuity is brought to bear. Of this, I was also painfully aware.

From another point of view, a church is the house of God. For Catholics, that means a place where the Blessed Sacrament is kept in a precious safe, called a tabernacle, on a permanent table of sacrifice, called an altar. It is the actual dwelling place of Jesus Christ in our midst. But not the Assembly Hall; its very nature makes the reservation of the Holy Sacrament of the Altar impossible. Its very nature also makes it impossible to have pews, kneeling benches, Stations of the Cross, statues, confessionals, and a baptismal font. People can assemble anywhere and worship God. They can certainly do it in an assembly hall. But they can do it better in a place intended exclusively for divine worship, a church which, by its very nature, is the house of God.

I had not gathered my new flock about me very many times before I arrived at a decision. I decided that my flock needed a chapel—a full-fledged, full-size, honest-to-goodness church. Not a little gem like the chapel in my residence, which could accommodate only 5 percent of my congregation, or even a spacious chamber like the auditorium in the projected new Education Building, which would accommodate only 50 percent of our liturgy. The little chapel is fine as far as it goes; so will the spanking new auditorium be someday. But the little chapel does not go far enough spatially, and no auditorium could ever go far enough ecclesiastically.

The special prayers we were saying every Sunday for our friends, relatives, and benefactors had been extended to include those who died during the preceding week. Now another intention was added: "For our new chapel." We began asking God to grant us the means by which we could build a proper house in which to worship Him more properly. The people of God for whom this institution is either their lifelong community or their training ground for the community outside, for whom this school is really their parish, began to dream of gathering together in love of God in the same sort of place used by the rest of God's people for divine worship—a church of their own.

Prayers are quickly said, and dreams are easily dreamed. But the prayers are not always so quickly answered, and the dreams not so easily fulfilled. Nor are churches built with dream blocks and spiritual cement. The hard materials of construction demand a similar commodity—hard cash. Considerations of higher finance could never be appreciated by my congregation, but they were all too obvious to me.

I was fully aware that the State, committed as it is to decisive separation from the Church, could not appropriate one cent for the construction of a religious edifice. In fact, our state has taken care to establish that point in black and white in its *Policy Manual*. That does not mean that institution chapels are officially frowned on. The *Policy Man-*

ual specifically makes provisions for their erection, even to the use of state land if it is available. But the construction must be done by a religious corporation, which must provide the hard materials—and the hard cash.

Normally the religious corporation needed to build a church is the parish and the providers of the hard cash are the parishioners. I had to say that to myself only once in order to realize that my parish is not incorporated and the hardest thing to get from my parishioners would be cash. Praying comes much easier to the retarded than money, but money can be prayed for, too. In fact, many of the saints found that as a means of securing money, praying for it is second only to earning it. I soon realized that in praying for our new chapel, my patients were essentially praying for money, which happens to be the root of at least some good. I also realized, however, that many of the boys and girls have some actual earning power and many others receive spending money from relatives and friends. They could not begin to pay for their own chapel, of course. But if they could buy candy and pop and cigarettes, they could save a dime, a nickel, or at least a penny every week. Why could we not have a Sunday collection?

We could. We did. The pennies and nickels and dimes began pouring in. In the course of a year my patients contributed more than $500 to the church—in itself an insignificant sum. But the lessons learned are worth a great deal more than the actual cash value. Now my congregation knows that it costs money to provide the material requisites for divine worship and that they have a part in making that provision. They have learned how to undertake little sacrifices in order to play that part.

But most of all, they understand why "just praying won't make it so"; they know the chief reason why they will have to pray hard and long before our new chapel can become a reality. They could never comprehend the many other complications which would delay the accomplishment of that reality. But a single reason is sufficient for the retarded to see why their prayers are not immediately answered. Most of them are able to comprehend that reason better since the inauguration of the Sunday collection. As a result, their prayers for our dream church will cease only when they can say their prayers in our *real* church.

XIX

THE INSIDE STORY

MEANWHILE, back at the Assembly Hall, variety continued to spice the lives of our patients. Jewish ritual, Protestant worship, and Catholic devotions will probably be sandwiched in between dances, movies, parties, gym classes, and an assortment of other events for many a moon. But that is life—at least in an institution—the kind of life to which I had become accustomed.

Accustomed? Yes, the months into which the weeks and days had grown were themselves growing into years. As I look back now on those first days and weeks, they seem as unreal as ever—but in a reversed sort of way. While I was living them, the whole new world into which I had stepped seemed to be unreal. But now, in retrospect, *I* am the one who appears to be the only unrealistic feature in the picture. Today I wonder how the people and places and things which are such a common, ordinary part of my environment could ever have seemed strange to me.

I often think of how staggered I was that first day by

the size and number of the buildings. Now I am amused to hear others express such awe when I accompany them on a tour of the institution. And yet I have seen enough bricks laid since that day to encircle the earth a few more times. For in these short years our very inadequate Storehouse, Laundry Building, and Powerhouse have been replaced by huge new structures. Even the "private park" in front of my residence has long since succumbed to the bulldozer, the roadway has moved back a hundred feet, and the two "swimming pools" have disappeared under a modern architectural wonder of brick and glass, which will soon begin to function as our new Education Building. I am not unimpressed by the size and number of our buildings, but neither am I overwhelmed as I once was. Now that the State School and I are part of each other, I not only see but even feel the need for the buildings of yesterday and today and even of tomorrow. Indeed I insist that we still need at least *one* more building everytime the Assembly Hall becomes a church.

I also laugh many times now at the nonchalance of which I accused my predecessor as he took me for a jaunt around the grounds. Our 519 acres have not shrunk a bit since that first visit of mine, but my estimate of them has certainly contracted. It is still a big place—there is no doubt about it—but today it seems impossible to me that anyone should have to be rescued by a patrolman and escorted from the Front to the Moss. Everytime I see Jim Meath, I think of how lost I must have looked that day.

And I think of the merry-go-round. All the things that then appeared to be swimming in circles at such breakneck speed look so static now: wards, dayrooms, dormitories, mountains of laundry—and that little foreign car flitting from one spot to another. Now my own little foreign car seems as native and natural and normal as the dormitories, dayrooms, and wards, and the heaps of laundry impress me only as foothills.

I can still see myself groping through the mysterious depths of my new office like the skin diver making his first acquaintance with the denizens of the deep. Or perhaps even more like the fish itself—*out* of water. Now these office items are as close to me as scales to the fish. I have long since solved all the mysteries in this chamber of secrets—and added to them, ensuring that my successor will indeed have reason to be mystified.

When I recall the host of ugly adjectives that crowded into my mind as I was approaching the Hill for the first time, I wonder how I could have been so ignorant and naïve. If I had known at that time that the place was fondly called the Hill, I am sure I would have read the "i" for "e" and the fondness for folly. Now that I have personally acquired that fondness, I am embarrassed to admit that I was the one with the monopoly on the folly.

How could I have been so numb and dumb? Of course, I had a lot to learn. It is understandable why I was so mentally deficient about mental deficiency. But why did the prospect petrify me and strike me thoughtless and speechless? Heaven knows, I have thought and spoken my share ever since. I often think now how grateful everyone else here would undoubtedly be if I would just keep quiet for a while—and even if I would stop thinking at times. But in my hour of numbness and dumbness my Bishop would have appreciated a little cerebral and verbal activity on my part—a consideration which makes me ever more grateful for His Excellency's patience during my days of indecision.

Yes, my reveries often cause me to gaze in amazement at that bewildered, befuddled, besweated greenhorn who took the reins of the Catholic Chaplaincy here seven years ago. What a spectacle he must have presented to the other people!

The other people—thank God for the other people! Not one of them ever let on. No one ever laughed as I stumbled and fumbled. No one ever treated me like a greenhorn, although everyone pitched in and helped in the ripening process. Even the patients. Their spokesman gave me a hearty welcome that first Sunday morning. And Ted— what a help he was in those early days! I think of how he baffled me at first. Now I know him like a book. And how miffed I was by those early encounters with some of the other patients and their problems! But there were always people to set me straight.

When I stop to think of it now, the matter seems utterly different. Underlying all the numbness and dumbness, the bewilderment and befuddlement, the ignorance and naïveté was really the basic emotion of fear. I was scared! The number and size of the buildings, the extent of the grounds, the unfamiliarity of the jargon, the strangeness of the surroundings, the mysterious atmosphere, the awesome responsibility—all this is enough to scare the daylights out of anybody.

Nevertheless, as I look back now, I see that the real cause of my fear was the people. I remember how curious I was about many things, like the buildings, but my overriding concern was not the inanimate objects. I remember that my real fear crystallized when I approached the first ward with my guide and realized that we were going indoors—where the patients were.

There is no doubt about it: I was terrified at the very thought of this segment of humanity. And the severity of my apprehension was scarcely less in regard to the other part of the institution's population: the personnel. To the uninitiated, facing 4,000 retarded children hardly presents a more formidable prospect than surveying 1,000 assorted psychiatrists, psychologists, therapists, pathologists, psychiatric aides, and various others whose specialties are as confined to institutions as those whom they treat.

Truthfully, what is more terrifying to people than people? We expect members of other species to be quite different from ourselves. The thought of a marine octopus is not nearly as unpleasant as the thought of a human octopus. John Doe is horrified at the growl of a bear, but disgust is added to horror when John Doe's boss is a bear. The less people are like people, the more awesome they become.

As I drove up the hill on that sweltering June day seven years ago, I was not expecting to see any human octopuses or bears within these walls, to be sure. Nevertheless, I was doing the inhabitants an injustice, because I feared them, both patients and personnel. I really did not know what to expect, but I must have entertained a vague suspicion that they all might be at least slightly removed from the human species. And I was afraid.

Now I feel as foolish as the running child who sees that

his threatening shadow disappears as soon as he gets directly under the light. Under the direct light of experience all my fears have faded away. Like the little boy and his shadow, I have discovered that the humanity of both personnel and patients merges with my own in the rays of that light. How different it looks from the *inside!* People on the Outside will never really understand a place like this. But I hope they stand a better chance—now that I have turned it inside out.